Bac Pro 2de

A2-B1

W0367431

PRO TIP TOP ENGLISH

F. Bascou, professeure d'anglais au lycée polyvalent Alfred Kastler, Talence (33)
J. Herter, professeure d'anglais au lycée des Métiers Émile Baudot, Wassy (52)
B. Léonori, professeure d'anglais honoraire
S. Ritter, IEN Anglais-Lettres, académie de Reims
É. Rumburg, professeure d'anglais au lycée professionnel Le Champ de Claye, Claye-Souilly (77)
S. Vitel, professeure d'anglais au lycée polyvalent Jean Hanzelet, Pont-à-Mousson (54)

FOUCHER

LES LIENS FOUCHERCONNECT

Le manuel papier s'enrichit de ressources numériques

foucherconnect.fr

GRATUIT !
Accessible **SANS INSCRIPTION.**
EN LIGNE sur www.foucherconnect.fr

▶ **Des pictogrammes** indiquent au fil des pages les liens vers les ressources en ligne.

Exemple :

Soit

J'accède à la ressource *via* l'adresse complète www.foucherconnect.fr/21ptt01

Soit

J'accède à la ressource *via* la plateforme www.foucherconnect.fr

J'enregistre cette page dans mes favoris pour mes prochaines visites.

Je saisis **le code de la ressource** indiqué dans le pictogramme.

▶ **Des flashcodes** vous permettent aussi d'accéder à certaines ressources avec un smartphone ou une tablette.

Conception graphique	Anne-Danielle Naname
Adaptation maquette et mise en page	Bénédicte Chantalou, Yuruga
Iconographie	Katia Davidoff
Relecture	Victoria Britten
Illustration	Sara Lomuscio

ISBN 978-2-216-16172-0

Sommaire

UNIT 1

Are You a Gamer? p. 9

- **The Setting and the Plot** p. 10
  - A2 **Action 1** Rédiger une brève description d'un jeu vidéo p. 11
- **Customize Your Character** p. 12
  - A2 **Action 2** Décrire un personnage de jeu vidéo à partir d'une liste de points p. 13
- **Differentiated Activities** p. 14
- **Training** p. 15
- **Project** A2 Imagine a Video Game p. 17
- **AP** Prendre la parole en continu p. 18

Grammaire
la possession (*have*, les déterminants possessifs), la capacité (*can*), l'auxiliaire *be*, *There is / There are*
Phonologie
la terminaison « s » du pluriel

UNIT 2

How to Survive in London p. 19

- **First Contacts with the Host Family** p. 20
  - A2 **Action 1** Écrire une description brève d'une première journée à l'étranger p. 21
- **Visiting London** p. 22
  - A2 **Action 2** Demander des informations sur une attraction londonienne p. 23
- **Differentiated Activities** p. 24
- **Training** p. 25
- **Project** A2 Create a Survival Kit for a Trip in an English-speaking Country p. 27
- **AP** Prendre part à une conversation p. 28

Grammaire
le présent simple, la construction des questions, l'heure digitale
Phonologie
les sons /w/ et /h/ dans les mots interrogatifs

CULTURE CLICK 1 **Space Exploration** p. 29

UNIT 3

How to Make the Most of an Internship p. 31

Show Your Personality p. 32

A2+ **Action 1** Donner des conseils sur l'attitude à adopter en stage p. 33

Dress Code and Safety p. 34

A2+ **Action 2** Dire ce qu'on doit porter sur le lieu de travail MÉDIATION p. 34

A2 **Action 3** Écrire des conseils sur la sécurité au travail p. 35

Differentiated Activities p. 36

Training p. 37

Project A2+ Create a Tutorial for Future Interns p. 39

AP Comprendre un document audio ou vidéo p. 40

Grammaire
l'impératif,
le conseil (*should*),
l'obligation (*must*),
l'interdiction (*mustn't*)
Phonologie
les syllabes accentuées

UNIT 4

Be Sporty! p. 41

Top Level Tournaments p. 42

A1 **Action 1** Écrire des phrases simples sur le thème du sport p. 42

A2 **Action 2** Donner des explications sur des projets futurs p. 43

Sports for Life p. 44

A1 **Action 3** Écrire des phrases sur des actions en cours p. 45

Differentiated Activities p. 46

Training p. 47

Project A2+ Create an Interactive Quiz about Sport p. 49

AP Comprendre un document écrit p. 50

Grammaire
le futur,
le présent en *-ing*
Phonologie
la lettre « u »

CULTURE CLICK 2 **The FBI** p. 51

UNIT 5 Essential Workers Needed p. 53

- Frontline Jobs p. 54
  - A2 Action 1 Rédiger un paragraphe donnant un aperçu d'un métier p. 54
  - A2 Action 2 Comprendre des informations sur un métier p. 55
- Jobs That Serve the Community p. 56
  - A2+ Action 3 Donner un avis sur un métier p. 57
- Differentiated Activities p. 58
- Training p. 59
- Project A2+ Post a Job Description p. 61
- **AP** Interagir à l'écrit p. 62

Grammaire
Les articles indéfinis *a* / *an* / ∅, les verbes modaux *can* et *may*
Phonologie
la lettre « a »

UNIT 6 Looking at the Past p. 63

- Periods Full of Surprises p. 64
  - A2 Action 1 Donner des informations sur des événements passés p. 65
- Years of Environmental Issues p. 66
  - B1 Action 2 Rassembler des informations de sources différentes et les résumer pour quelqu'un d'autre MÉDIATION p. 67
- Differentiated Activities p. 68
- Training p. 69
- Project A2+ Present a Slide Show about Past Events p. 71
- **AP** Présenter un projet p. 72

Grammaire
les dates,
les prépositions,
le prétérit (forme affirmative)
Phonologie
les dates

CULTURE CLICK 3 Her Majesty Queen Elizabeth II p. 73

UNIT 7 Back from My Internship p. 75

- In the Workplace p. 76
  - A2 **Action 1** Poser des questions sur un stage et y répondre p. 77
- Getting the Best out of Work Experience p. 78
  - A2+ **Action 2** Faire une description brève des bénéfices d'un stage p. 79
- Differentiated Activities p. 80
- Training p. 81

Project A2+ Record a Presentation of Your Work Placement and Discuss It p. 83

- **AP** Répondre à des questions p. 84

Grammaire
le prétérit (forme interrogative et négative / *be*), *There was / There were*
Phonologie
les sons /ɜː/ et /eə/

UNIT 8 Customer Satisfaction p. 85

- Treat Yourself! p. 86
  - A2 **Action 1** Présenter et donner son opinion sur une prestation de service p. 87
- Dealing with Commercial Problems p. 88
  - A2 **Action 2** Comprendre une conversation téléphonique à propos d'une commande p. 88
  - A2 **Action 3** Rédiger un commentaire de consommateur p. 89
- Differentiated Activities p. 90
- Training p. 91

Project A2+ Make a Phone Complaint p. 93

- **AP** Répondre à une plainte p. 94

Grammaire
les verbes de sentiment, les nombres
Phonologie
les sons /ai/ et /ei/

CULTURE CLICK 4 Evolution of Music in the United States p. 95

UNIT 9 Social Networks and Teens p. 97

- The Use of Social Media p. 98
  - A2+ Action 1 Poser et répondre à des questions sur l'utilisation des réseaux sociaux p. 99
- Social Media: Friend or Enemy? p. 100
  - B1 Action 2 Résumer des informations factuelles sur les dangers des réseaux sociaux p. 101
- Differentiated Activities p. 102
- Training p. 103
- Project B1 Conduct a Survey About Social Networks p. 105
- AP Réagir à une problématique à l'écrit p. 106

Grammaire
les adverbes de fréquence (*always, often, never*...), les indicateurs de fréquence, les données chiffrées
Phonologie
la lettre « c »

UNIT 10 Powerful Women in History p. 107

- First Fights p. 108
  - A2+ Action 1 Donner des informations sur des événements passés p. 109
- Wind of Change... p. 110
  - B1 Action 2 Comprendre une présentation p. 111
- Differentiated Activities p. 112
- Training p. 113
- Project B1 Present an Inspirational Woman p. 115
- AP Justifier ses choix p. 116

Grammaire
la permission et l'interdiction au passé, le prétérit *vs* le *present perfect*
Phonologie
le son /ʊ/

CULTURE CLICK 5 Scary Creatures p. 117

Annexes p. 119

VERS LE CCF

Présentation de l'épreuve p. 120

Vers le CCF 1
Compréhension de l'oral – Compréhension de l'écrit p. 122
Expression écrite p. 123

Vers le CCF 2
Compréhension de l'oral – Compréhension de l'écrit p. 124
Expression écrite p. 125

Vers le CCF 3
Compréhension de l'oral – Compréhension de l'écrit p. 126
Expression écrite p. 127

UNIT 1

Are You a Gamer?

PROJECT A2

You participate in a video game contest in your school. Imagine a video game and present it to the class, who will vote for the best game.

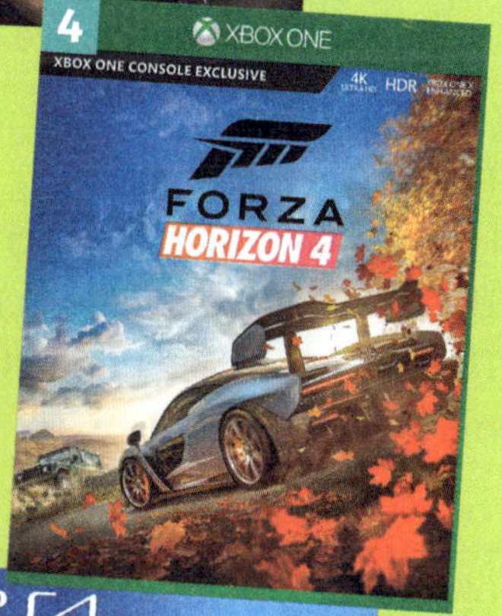

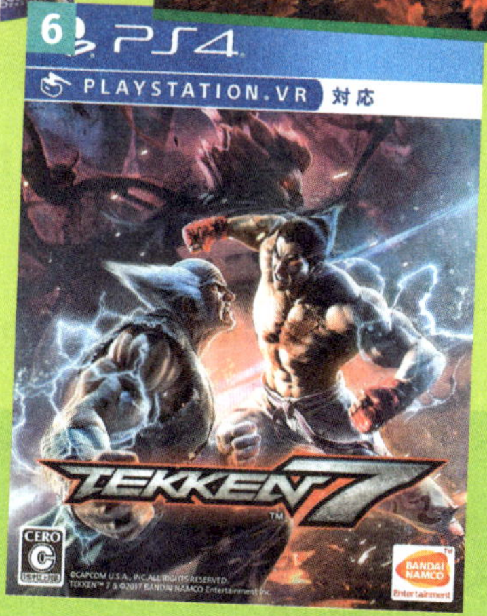

1 01 **Match the pictures and the genres. Listen and check.**

a. a fighting game ....

b. a sports game ....

c. a racing game ....

d. a role-playing game ....

e. a strategy game ....

f. a battle royale and shooting game ....

2 **Say if you like video games and what your favourite type of game is.**

FLIPPED CLASSROOM

Find the words corresponding to the following definitions.

a. A person in a story, in a film or in a game: ....

b. The place and the time in which an action takes place: ....

c. The story of a film, a book or a game: ....

d. Clothes for a particular occasion: ....

e. What you see in an area: mountains, lakes, houses...: ....

1'30"
CAPSULE
Are You a Gamer?
foucherconnect.fr/21ptt01

UNIT 1 The Setting and the Plot

ACTIVITY A Into the Future

LET'S GO FURTHER !!! →p. 14

1 (02) **Listen and tick the correct answer.**

Genre	☐ action role-playing ☐ strategy
Place of the action	☐ on Earth ☐ in another galaxy
Period	☐ in the 21st century ☐ in the 22nd century
Description of the galaxy	☐ 5 worlds ☐ 7 worlds
	☐ 100 planets ☐ 1000 planets
Name of the ship	☐ Andromeda ☐ Tempest
Role of the player	☐ a military recruit ☐ a citizen*
Objective	☐ to find a new home for humanity ☐ to destroy other planets

* *un citoyen*

WORD BOX

- **find*** trouver
- **a hill** une colline
- **an island** une île
- **an office** un bureau
- **a ship** un vaisseau, un navire
- **take* place** avoir lieu, se dérouler
- **a world** un monde

2 **Use the elements above to present *Mass Effect Andromeda* orally.**

a. (...) is an (...) video game.
b. The action takes place (...), (...).
c. In the galaxy, there are (...) and (...).
d. The name of the ship is (...).
e. The player has the role of (...).
f. His objective is (...).

GRAMMAR SPOT

a. There is a desert.
b. There are three different zones.

→ *Les éléments soulignés se traduisent par: ....*

→ *« There is » est suivi d'un nom au :* ☐ *singulier* ☐ *pluriel*

→ *« There are » est suivi d'un nom au :* ☐ *singulier* ☐ *pluriel*

Training ex. 5 p. 15

ACTIVITY B Different Landscapes

1 (03) **Listen and complete the labels.**

schools • islands • a desert • valleys • hospitals • beaches • fire stations • lakes • a forest • apartment buildings • shops • offices • hills • farms

a 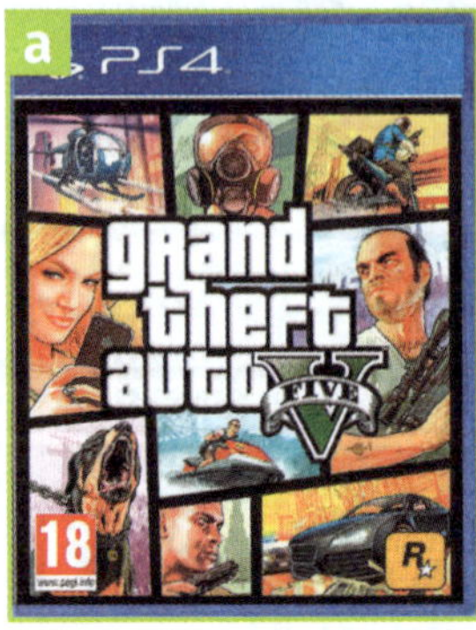

....
....
....
....
....
....
....

b 

....
....
....
....
....
....
....

2 **Say what there is or are in each video game.**

(In ... there is/are ...).

ACTIVITY C

An Action Role-playing Video Game

Synopsis

Horizon Zero Dawn takes place in the 31st century, in a post-apocalyptic world where colossal machines dominate the land. Human civilization has regressed to tribal societies of hunters and gatherers[1] who survive in immense forests, imposing mountain ranges, and the atmospheric ruins of their ancestors.

The player controls Aloy, a huntress who uses her speed, cunning[2], and agility to stay alive and protect her tribe against the force, size, and power of the machines.

https://horizon.fandom.com.

1. *des chasseurs-cueilleurs*; 2. *la ruse, l'ingéniosité*

1 **Orally describe the picture using *"I can see, there is, there are"*.**

2 **Tick True or False and justify your answers.**

a. Horizon Zero Dawn is set in the future. ☐ True ☐ False ....

b. Machines control this post-apocalyptic world. ☐ True ☐ False ....

c. The action takes place in a city landscape. ☐ True ☐ False ....

3 **Find the English equivalents in paragraph 2.**

a. *une chasseresse*: ....

b. *utiliser*: ....

c. *sa vitesse*: ....

d. *rester en vie*: ....

e. *sa tribu*: ....

f. *contre*: ....

GRAMMAR SPOT

a. **He is a recruit. <u>His</u> objective is to find a new home.**

b. **She protects <u>her</u> tribe.**

Les déterminants possessifs soulignés font référence à :

– Phrase a : ☐ *un homme* ☐ *une femme*

– Phrase b : ☐ *un homme* ☐ *une femme*

Training ex. 8 p. 16

4 **Answer the questions.**

a. Who is the character in the video game?

....

....

b. What is her role?

....

WORD BOX

- **a castle** un château
- **a daughter** une fille
- **mountain ranges** des chaînes de montagnes

ACTION 1

Rédiger une brève description d'un jeu vidéo

A2

Use the elements below to write a short paragraph to describe the video game *The Witcher 3*.

→ **Genre** = action role-playing
→ **Setting** = a fantasy world / different regions / mountains, forests, castles
→ **Main character** = Geralt of Rivia, called "the Witcher", who is a monster hunter
→ **Secondary characters** = humans, nonhumans, elves, monsters
→ **Objective** = find the emperor's daughter

Customize Your Character

ACTIVITY D A World Record Breaker

WORD BOX
- **a braid** une natte
- **fly*** voler
- **jump** sauter
- **a ponytail** une queue de cheval
- **prevent** empêcher
- **travel** voyager
- **a treasure** un trésor

1 04 **Listen and complete.**

Character	Game	Nationality
....	....	....

2 04 **Listen again and tick what you hear.**

a. Her job: ☐ a soldier ☐ an archaeologist ☐ a treasure hunter
b. Her personality: ☐ powerful ☐ athletic ☐ brave ☐ intelligent ☐ sporty ☐ determined
c. Her appearance: ☐ brown eyes ☐ blue eyes ☐ brown hair ☐ black hair ☐ a braid ☐ a ponytail

3 05 **Fill in the labels with the following words. Listen and check.**

Her outfit: a tank top • shorts • combat boots • socks
Her accessories: fingerless gloves • a utility belt • pistols

4 **Present the character orally.**

GRAMMAR SPOT

a. She has brown hair. b. She is athletic.
Dans la phrase a, le verbe utilisé est : ☐ *être* ☐ *avoir*
Dans la phrase b, le verbe utilisé est : ☐ *être* ☐ *avoir*
c. You can teleport to work.
Qu'exprime « can » ? ....
De quoi est-il suivi ? ....

Training ex. 6, 7, 8 p. 16

ACTIVITY E What Can He Do?

1 **Watch the beginning of the video to 0:15 and complete.**

His name is .... The video is about the five coolest .... in ....

2 **Watch the end of the video and number the superpowers in the order you hear them.**

...... teleportation ...... gravity control ...... electricity ...... time control ...... eagle vision

3 **Watch again and match the abilities and the powers.**

a. With power n°1, you can •	• 1. prevent bad things from happening.
b. With power n°2, you can •	• 2. jump super high and you can fly.
c. With power n°3, you can •	• 3. look through walls.
d. With power n°4, you can •	• 4. teleport to work or school or travel anywhere in the world.
e. With power n°5, you can •	• 5. shoot electricity.

ACTIVITY F Inspired by Peter Pan

STEP BY STEP →p. 14

1 Read the text and fill in the appropriate subtitles.

abilities • appearance • personality

Link is the main protagonist of the *Legend of Zelda* series. [...]. The various heroes who use the name Link are courageous young boys or teenagers, often in green clothing, who leave their homes to save the world from evil forces. [...]

....

He usually has light-colored hair (ranging from brown to blonde to orange), blue eyes and a medium build. [...] In promotional material for *Breath of the Wild*, Link wears the Champion's Tunic and a simple pair of Hylian Trousers. [...]

....

He is implied to be somewhat[1] sleepy or lazy. [...] Link possesses basic characteristics found in a heroic character: bravery, compassion, determination, and wisdom[2]. [...]

....

Link is remarkably proficient with a wide variety of weapons, instruments, and other items, being able to use them immediately upon obtaining them[3]. His preferred weapons of choice though, are swords. In each of his adventures, Link's primary form of combat becomes sword fighting, usually with a shield.

https://zelda.fandom.com.

1. *on sous-entend qu'il est un peu;* 2. *la sagesse;* 3. *quand il les obtient*

2 Find the equivalents.

a. *des adolescents* (§1): ....

b. *les forces du mal* (§1): ....

c. *une carrure moyenne* (§2): ....

d. *paresseux* (§3): ....

e. *des armes* (§4): ....

f. *des épées* (§4): ....

3 Complete the grid about the character.

Name	....
Game	....
Mission	....
Physical description	....

Outfit	....
Qualities	....
Weapons	....

ACTION 2

Décrire un personnage de jeu vidéo à partir d'une liste de points

A2

Orally describe this character.

→ **Name** = Mario
→ **Physical description** = small, a moustache
→ **Outfit** = blue overalls, a red cap, white gloves
→ **Personality** = impulsive, brave
→ **Abilities** = throw fireballs, fly in the air

Differentiated Activities

LET'S GO FURTHER!!!

ACTIVITY A

p. 10

2'14"
VIDÉO
Returnal - Announcement Trailer
foucherconnect.fr/21ptt03

1 Watch the video and circle the correct elements.

a. The game is a (*racing* / *shooting* / *strategy*) video game.
b. The action takes place (*in the past* / *in the present* / *in the future*).
c. The main character is a middle-aged (*man* / *woman*).
d. The character fights (*spiders* / *creatures*).

2 Tick True or False.

a. The character is a pilot. ☐ True ☐ False
b. The character uses a space ship. ☐ True ☐ False
c. The landscape is composed of beaches and lakes. ☐ True ☐ False
d. The planet is different every time she dies. ☐ True ☐ False

3 Watch again and fill in the blanks.

a. Over and over I relive my first moments on this .... planet: the crash, the ...., my death.
b. Trapped in this endless cycle, even death is no ....
c. This .... is becoming part of me, infecting my mind, my memories.
d. But I .... lose hope. My only choice is to keep ....

STEP BY STEP

ACTIVITY F

p. 13

1 Read the text and fill in the appropriate subtitles.

abilities • appearance • personality

2 Match the equivalents.

a. *des adolescents* (§1) •
b. *les forces du mal* (§1) •
c. *une carrure moyenne* (§2) •
d. *paresseux* (§3) •
e. *des armes* (§4) •
f. *des épées* (§4) •

• 1. weapons
• 2. a medium build
• 3. swords
• 4. lazy
• 5. teenagers
• 6. evil forces

3 Tick the correct answers.

a. ☐ Peter Pan ☐ Link is the main character of the *Legend of Zelda* series.
b. His mission is: ☐ to kill humans ☐ to save the world from evil forces
c. He has: ☐ light-colored hair ☐ dark hair and: ☐ green eyes ☐ blue eyes
d. His qualities are: ☐ bravery ☐ speed ☐ compassion ☐ determination ☐ wisdom

4 Fill in the labels with:

tunic • hair • trousers • eyes • sword • shield

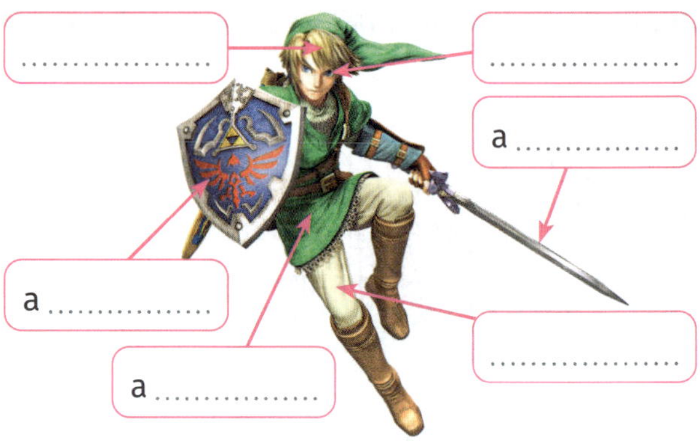

AUDIO foucherconnect.fr/21ptt04

EXERCICES INTERACTIFS foucherconnect.fr/21ptt05

in TUNE

A 06 **Écoutez et répétez les mots au pluriel. /s/** sports - **/z/** cars - **/iz/** forces

B 07 **Placez les mots suivants dans la bonne colonne, puis écoutez et vérifiez.**

houses • shorts • farms • boots • beaches • offices • castles • humans • lakes

/s/	/z/	/iz/
....	....	....

1 08 **Remettez les lettres dans l'ordre pour retrouver des lieux ou des paysages. Écoutez et vérifiez.**

a. LIHL = H..........
b. ONTIAMUN = M..........
c. VLYAEL = V..........
d. SETRFO = F..........
e. RODWL = W..........
f. LAPNTE = P..........
g. TERDSE = D..........

2 09 **Écrivez les mots correspondant aux images. Puis écoutez et vérifiez.**

			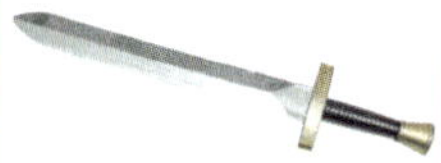
a.	b.	c.	d. ....
	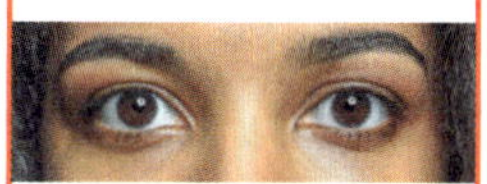		
e.	f.	g.	h. ....

3 **Complétez avec les mots ci-dessous.**

character • settings • outfit • centuries • abilities

a. Kassandra is the main .... of the series *Assassin's Creed*.
b. There are different ....: Ancient Egypt, Ancient Greece, the French Revolution...
c. The action takes place in different places and different ....
d. Kassandra has many .... thanks to her weapon.
e. Her .... is composed of a belt, boots and an armour.

4 **Challenge!**

Vous avez deux minutes pour lister autant de genres et de noms de jeux vidéo que possible.

5 **Complétez avec *there is* ou *there are*.**

a. .... a game I really love; it is called *Fortnite*.
b. .... three different game modes.
c. .... a Battle Royale mode; it is a free game.
d. .... a player-versus-player game.
e. .... many characters.
f. .... millions of players.

6 **Conjuguez le verbe *be* au présent à la forme affirmative (+) ou négative (–).**

a. I .... fond of video games. (+)
b. My favourite game .... Minecraft. (+)
c. The landscape .... incredible. (+)
d. We .... video game addicts! (+)
e. The game .... difficult. (-)
f. The characters .... very funny. (+)
g. But they .... realistic. (-)
h. The plot .... interesting. (-)

7 **Complétez avec *is* ou *has*.**

a. Who .... your favourite character?
b. He .... short brown hair.
c. He .... intelligent and courageous.
d. He .... blue eyes.
e. He .... young.
f. He .... a beautiful outfit.

8 **Observez les deux cartes ci-contre puis entourez les bonnes réponses.**

a. (*His / Her*) name is Kratos. (*His / Her*) name is Athena.
b. (*His / Her*) main weapons are blades and an axe. (*His / Her*) weapons are swords.
c. (*His / Her*) mission is to spread his wife's ashes[1]. (*His / Her*) mission is to liberate mankind[2] with the power of hope.
d. Athena (*can / can't*) create weapons, but she (*can / can't*) become invisible.

1. répandre les cendres de sa femme; 2. l'humanité

Name: Kratos
Weapons: blades, an axe
Example of abilities: manipulate time
Mission: to spread his wife's ashes

Name: Athena
Weapons: swords
Example of abilities: create weapons
Mission: to liberate mankind with the power of hope

TIPS — LANGUAGE

La possession

have

I have, you have, he/she/it has, we have, they have

He has a ship. *Il a un vaisseau.*

They have weapons. *Ils ont des armes.*

les déterminants possessifs

My, your, his/her/its, our, your, their

Her name is Zelda. *Son nom est Zelda.*

His name is Link. *Son nom est Link.*

La capacité ou l'incapacité

Pour dire ce que l'on peut ou sait faire (ou pas)

can + V ou can't + V

He can throw fireballs. *Il peut jeter des boules de feu.*

He can't fly. *Il ne peut pas voler.*

L'auxiliaire *be*

Pour exprimer un état

Forme affirmative

I am/I'm
he/she/it is/'s
we/you/they are/'re

I am a real fan. *Je suis un vrai fan.*

Forme négative

I am not/I'm not
He/she/it is not/isn't
We/you/they are not/aren't

Forme interrogative

Am I ...?
Is he/she/it ...?
Are we/you/they ...?

Pour traduire « il y a »

***There is* + singulier**

There is a lake. *Il y a un lac.*

***There are* + pluriel**

There are castles. *Il y a des châteaux.*

UNIT 1

PROJECT

A2

Imagine a Video Game

SCENARIO

Vous participez à un concours sur les jeux vidéo organisé dans votre lycée. Imaginez le contexte du jeu et le personnage principal, puis présentez-les à la classe qui élira le meilleur concept de jeu.

A1

Écrire des expressions sur le lieu de vie d'un personnage

- Inventez le contexte du jeu et complétez la fiche ci-dessous.

→ Name of the game: ....

Genre: ....

Time / period: ....

Place: ....

Landscape: ....

Secondary Characters: ....

Other details: ....

....

....

A1

Écrire des expressions sur un personnage imaginaire

- Inventez le personnage principal du jeu et complétez la fiche ci-dessous.

→ Name of the the main character: ....

Appearance → Physical description: ....

Outfit: ....

Personality: ....

Weapons: ....

Abilities: ....

Mission / objective: ....

Other details: ....

....

A2

Faire un bref exposé

- Entraînez-vous à prononcer les mots et expressions notés dans vos fiches.
- Vérifiez la prononciation des mots inconnus dans un dictionnaire en ligne.
- Présentez votre jeu vidéo et son personnage principal à la classe.
- Votez pour le concept de jeu que vous préférez parmi toutes les présentations.

Auto évaluation

PORTFOLIO

foucherconnect.fr/21ptt06

UNIT 1

Accompagnement Personnalisé — Prendre la parole en continu

Stratégies

1 Listez vos idées. Notez sous forme de notes tout ce que vous souhaitez dire, et faites des recherches, si nécessaire, pour compléter vos propos.

2 Organisez vos idées. Structurez vos idées (par exemple: introduction, développement, conclusion) grâce à quelques mots de liaison. A

3 Préparez-vous à faire des phrases. Faites des phrases courtes. Ne traduisez pas vos phrases sur Internet! Utilisez simplement les mots et expressions que vous connaissez. Soyez clair(e) dans vos propos. B

4 Soignez votre prononciation. Aidez-vous d'un dictionnaire en ligne ou d'Internet pour vérifier et améliorer votre prononciation. C

5 Osez prendre la parole. Restez calme et concentré(e). Parlez suffisamment fort et distinctement pour que votre auditoire vous comprenne.

Observation

1 (10) **Écoutez la présentation et complétez.**

I'm going to .... about John Price .... he is my favourite video game character. He is the main character in Call of Duty. First, I like his appearance and his personality. He is very tall. He has brown hair .... blue eyes. He has army clothing and he is serious. Then, I .... he is incredible. He is very strong. For ...., he can fight very well with his weapons. He is an excellent soldier. To conclude, in my ...., he is the best video game character!

2 **Entourez les trois éléments qui structurent la prise de parole.**

À vous de jouer !

Présentez oralement ce personnage de jeu vidéo en vous appuyant sur les éléments ci-dessous et en respectant les stratégies.

Name: Cloud Strife
Game: Final Fantasy VII
Personality: shy / loyal / kind
Appearance: young / spiky blond hair / blue eyes /an earring
Outfit: pants / a sleeveless shirt / a belt / brown boots
Weapon: a sword
Abilities: fight with swords / ride a motorcycle and a snowboard

À retenir

A Pour structurer une prise de parole	B Pour expliquer un propos	C Services convertissant un texte en fichier audio
– first *d'abord*	– but *mais*	www.fromtexttospeech.com
– then/next *puis/ensuite*	– for example *par exemple*	www.naturalreaders.com
– finally *finalement*	– because *parce que*	https://ttsreader.com
– to conclude *pour conclure*	– I think that... *je pense que...*	www.acapela-box.com
	– in my opinion *à mon avis*	

UNIT 2 How to Survive in London

PROJECT A2

You are going to spend a few days in a host family in an English-speaking country. Create a survival kit with useful sentences and vocabulary so you can communicate in different situations.

1 11 **Listen to the reasons why these students want to visit those places and complete.**

a. **Harrods:** I'm fond of ....

b. **Chelsea FC Stadium:** I'm very interested in ....

c. **The Shard:** I study architecture and I like modern ....

d. **London Dungeon:** I have a passion for ....

e. **Madame Tussauds:** I enjoy .... and I want to see my favourite stars.

2 **Match the pictures and the places listed in exercise 1.**

3 **What about you? What are you interested in?**

FLIPPED CLASSROOM

Find the words corresponding to the following definitions.

a. A family you stay with temporarily: ....

b. Something you can visit: ....

c. Breakfast, lunch, supper, dinner: ....

d. Food carried in a bag or box to work, to school or on an excursion: ....

e. Buses, planes, boats, cars, the Underground: ....

1'30"
CAPSULE
How to Survive in London
foucherconnect.fr/21ptt07

First Contacts with the Host Family

ACTIVITY A Introducing Yourself

STEP BY STEP → p. 24

1 (12) **Paul sends a voice message to his host family to present himself and his friend Alan before their arrival. Listen and find the missing information.**

a. The host mother is .... b. The host city is ....

c. Their departure is in .... weeks.

2 (12) **Listen again and find the correct information about Paul.**

a. Age: ....
b. Studies: ....

c. Place of living: a .... in the .... of ....

3 (12) **Listen again and answer the questions about Alan.**

a. How old is Alan? ....

b. Where does he live? ....

c. What does he study? ....

WORD BOX

- **a blanket** une couverture
- **live** habiter, vivre
- **a plug** une prise
- **a shower** une douche
- **stay** loger, séjourner
- **study** étudier
- **upstairs** à l'étage

GRAMMAR SPOT

a. I <u>study</u> photography. b. He <u>lives</u> in Reims.

→ *Ces verbes conjugués au présent simple expriment :* ☐ *une vérité générale* ☐ *une habitude* ☐ *un souhait*

→ *À quelle personne faut-il ajouter un « s » au verbe ?* ....

Training ex. 5, 6 & 7 p. 26

ACTIVITY B Visiting the House

1 **Fill in the labels with:**

kitchen • bedroom • bathroom • garden • living room

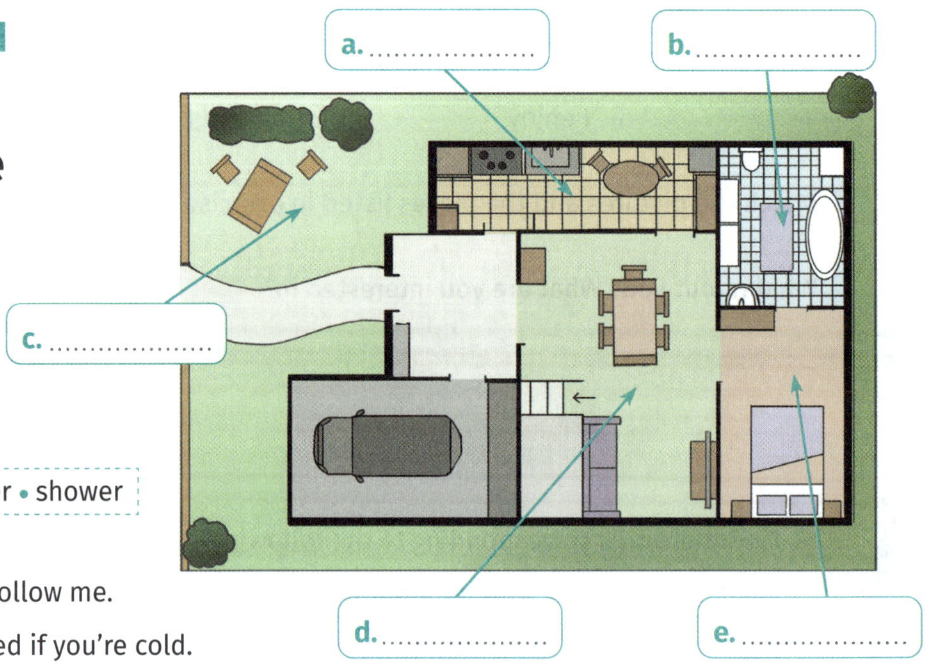

2 (13) **Complete with:**

blanket • fresh air • upstairs • adapter • shower

Then listen and check.

a. Your bedroom is .... Follow me.

b. There is a .... on the bed if you're cold.

c. The plugs are different in England, so this is an .... if you need to charge your phone.

d. You can have a .... in the morning or in the evening, as you wish.

e. If you want to get some ...., you can go in the garden.

ACTIVITY C Time for Dinner!

WORD BOX

- **breakfast** le petit-déjeuner
- **a can** une cannette
- **a pie** une tarte, une tourte
- **sweet** sucré
- **tomorrow** demain
- **vegetables** des légumes

1 14 **Listen and answer the questions.**

a. What is there for dinner? ....

b. What time is breakfast? ....

c. What drink do the boys like best for breakfast? ....

2 14 **Listen again and find the English equivalents.**

a. *le dîner est prêt* : .... ready

b. *tenez* : here ....

c. *bon appétit* : ....

d. *à demain* : .... tomorrow

GRAMMAR SPOT

Breakfast is at seven thirty.

Traduisez la phrase.

....

....

Comment fait-on pour donner l'heure digitale ?

....

....

Training ex. 1 p. 25

3 14 **Listen again and tick what their packed lunch is made up of.**

- ☐ vegetables
- ☐ a sandwich
- ☐ some fruit
- ☐ a chocolate bar
- ☐ a bag of crisps
- ☐ a yoghurt
- ☐ a can of soda
- ☐ a bottle of water

ACTIVITY D Good Morning!

VIDÉO 0'42"
Traditional Full English Breakfast
foucherconnect.fr/21ptt08

1 **Watch the video from the beginning to 0:08 and fill in the blanks.**

If you want to .... your day off right in ...., you have to start with a full English ....

2 **Fill in the labels with the words. Watch the video from 0:08 to 0:19 to check your answers.**

fried eggs • baked beans • hash brown • sausage • bacon • fried tomato • mushrooms

ACTION 1

A2 **Écrire une description brève d'une première journée à l'étranger**

Recap what you have understood about Paul and Alan's first day in London (the host family, the house, the typical food).

UNIT 2

Visiting London

ACTIVITY E

Famous Attractions

VIDÉO
1'41"
Top 10 Attractions London – UK Travel Guide
foucherconnect.fr/21ptt09

1 **Watch the video and write the names of the attractions.**

❶

The ....

❷

Buckingham Palace

❸

The ....

❹

....

❺

The ....

❻

Covent Garden

❼

A Thames river cruise

❽

A double-decker bus

❾

....

❿

....

2 **Watch again and tick "true" or "false".**

a. The video shows the top 10 attractions in England. ☐ true ☐ false
b. There are fountains in Trafalgar Square. ☐ true ☐ false
c. You can eat, drink and do some shopping at Covent Garden. ☐ true ☐ false
d. The Houses of Parliament are the residence of the monarch. ☐ true ☐ false
e. The London Eye is the symbol of the new millennium. ☐ true ☐ false

3 **Fill in the correct question word, then match the questions and the answers.**

a. .... is Trafalgar Square? • • 1. In 1894.
b. .... can you learn at the Tower of London? • • 2. The British monarch.
c. .... was Tower Bridge constructed? • • 3. Its many secrets.
d. .... lives at Buckingham Palace? • • 4. In central London.

ACTIVITY F A Royal Visit

LET'S GO FURTHER!!! → p. 24

www.visitlondon.com

Visit The State Rooms, Buckingham Palace

PRICES £

Adult	£26.50
Under 17	£14.50
Under 5	free

OPENING TIMES

Opening time	09:30
Last admission	16:15
Closing time	18:30

MAP & DIRECTIONS

By train	London Victoria
By bus	Bus numbers 11, 211
By Underground	Victoria, Green Park, Hyde Park Corner

BOOK TICKETS

1 Observe the document and answer the questions.

a. What can you visit at Buckingham Palace? ....

b. How much is a ticket for you? ....

c. What time does the Palace open? ....

d. How can you go there? ....

ACTIVITY G Going on Your Own

1 Fill in the labels with: bus • foot • taxi • Tube

a. I take the ....

b. I take the ....

c. I go by ....

d. I go on ....

2 (15) Listen and tick the correct answers.

a. Paul wants to visit: ☐ Tower Bridge ☐ the Tower of London

b. Alan wants to visit: ☐ Tower Bridge ☐ the Tower of London

c. The attractions are: ☐ close to each other ☐ far from each other

d. They can go: ☐ on foot ☐ by bus

e. If they get lost, they can: ☐ ask someone to tell them the way ☐ check the itinerary on a transport app

GRAMMAR SPOT

a. What time does the Palace open?

b. When can you visit the Palace?

L'ordre des mots dans ces questions est :

....

+ auxiliaire

+ ....

+ ....

(+ complément) + ?

Training ex. 8 p. 26

WORD BOX

- **close to** proche de
- **far from** loin de
- **get* lost** se perdre
- **the way** le chemin

ACTION 2

A2 Demander des informations sur une attraction londonienne

INTERNET foucherconnect.fr/21ptt10

Use the information to ask your partner 4 questions about a famous London attraction. Answer your partner's questions.

Differentiated Activities

STEP BY STEP

ACTIVITY A

p. 20

1 12 **Paul sends a voice message to his host family to introduce himself and his friend Alan before their arrival. Listen and circle the correct answer.**

a. The host mother is (*Poppy / Lucy*).

b. The host city is (*Reims / London*).

c. Their departure is in (*2 / 3*) weeks.

2 12 **Listen again and tick the correct information about Paul.**

a. Age: ☐ 14 ☐ 15 ☐ 16

b. Country of origin: ☐ Finland ☐ France

c. Place of living: ☐ a village ☐ a city

d. Studies: ☐ security ☐ forestry ☐ photography

3 12 **Listen again and fill in the blanks to answer the questions about Alan.**

a. How old is Alan? He is ....

b. Where does he live? He lives in ....

c. What does he study? He studies ....

LET'S GO FURTHER!!!

ACTIVITY F

p. 23

The Centrepiece of Britain's Constitutional Monarchy

Buckingham Palace is home to over 775 rooms; 19 of these are State rooms along with 52 official royal bedrooms and guest rooms. The staff themselves have an impressive 188 bedrooms, 92 offices and [...] 78 bathrooms.

Still very much a working building, it is the centrepiece of Britain's constitutional monarchy which includes the everyday duties of the Queen and the Duke of Edinburgh as well as their immediate family.

Buckingham Palace was first opened to the general public in 1993 and it is opened every year between April and September since.

https://buckinghampalace.co.uk.

1 **What is the name of the attraction?**

....

2 **Find the English equivalents in the document.**

a. *des pièces* (§1): ....

b. *des chambres d'amis* (§1): ....

c. *le personnel* (§1): ....

d. *les devoirs, les obligations* (§2): ....

3 **Answer the questions.**

a. How many rooms are there in the Palace? ....

b. When is the Palace open to the public? ....

4 **Tick True or False.**

a. The staff has 358 rooms in total. ☐ True ☐ False

b. The Queen works in the palace every day. ☐ True ☐ False

c. The palace was built in 1993. ☐ True ☐ False

Training

AUDIO
foucherconnect.fr/21ptt11

EXERCICES INTERACTIFS
foucherconnect.fr/21ptt12

in TUNE

A 16 **Écoutez la prononciation de ces mots interrogatifs puis répétez:** how – what

B 17 **Placez les mots interrogatifs dans la bonne colonne, puis écoutez et vérifiez.**

where • why • who • when • whose • which

/w/	/h/
....	....

1 18 **Écrivez ces horaires digitaux en toutes lettres. Écoutez et vérifiez.**

a. 8:15 = ...
b. 6:40 = ...
c. 12:30 = ...
d. 5:10 = ...
e. 7:25 = ...
f. 11:35 = ...
g. 3:45 = ...
h. 1:50 = ...

2 19 **Écrivez les mots correspondant aux images. Puis écoutez et vérifiez.**

a. ....

b. ....

c. ....

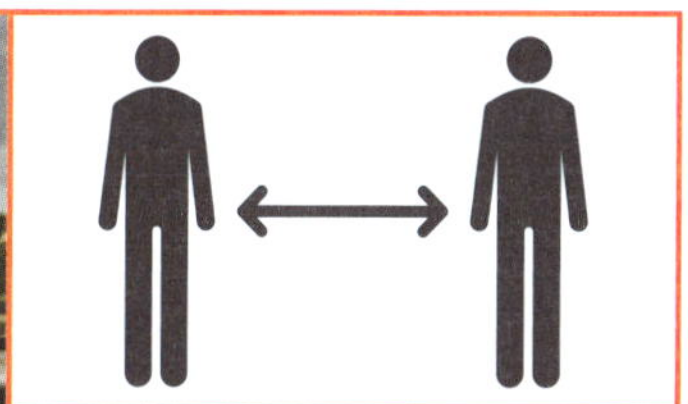
d. ....

e. ....

f. ....

g. ....

h. ....

3 **Complétez avec le mot qui convient:**

food • buildings • plugs • a packed lunch • shopping

a. In London, there are lots of modern ....
b. I really like ...., so Harrods is my favourite place!
c. Sausages and pies are typical .... in the United Kingdom.
d. The electrical .... are different in the UK.
e. Pupils often eat .... at school.

4 **Challenge!**

Vous avez deux minutes pour lister autant de lieux touristiques à Londres que possible.

TRAINING

5 **Réécrivez ces phrases à la troisième personne du singulier (« *he* » ou « *she* »).**

a. I live in England. ....

....

b. We don't work in a big company. ....

....

c. They study art. ....

d. You don't like visiting museums. ....

....

e. Do you take the bus? ....

....

6 **Conjuguez les verbes au présent simple.**

a. I .... to London every year. (*go*)

b. Generally, school .... at 3 or 4 in the afternoon. (*finish*)

c. She .... shopping in Oxford Street. (*love*)

d. They .... the bus to go to work. (*take*)

e. Amanda .... in a beautiful shop. (*work*)

7 **Conjuguez à la forme négative du présent simple.**

a. I .... going to the theatre. (*like*)

b. English people .... a typical breakfast every day. (*eat*)

c. The Prime Minister ....at Buckingham Palace but at 10 Downing Street. (*live*)

d. My sister ....art museums. (*enjoy*)

e. People ....in euros but in pounds. (*pay*)

8 **Posez les questions sur les parties soulignées.**

a. I go to school <u>by bus</u>.

....

b. The Shard is closed <u>on December 25th</u>.

....

c. I study <u>logistics</u>.

....

d. He likes London <u>because it is an incredible city</u>.

....

e. The London Eye is <u>close to Big Ben</u>.

....

TIPS

LANGUAGE

Le présent simple

Il s'utilise pour exprimer des actions habituelles ou des vérités générales.

Forme affirmative

***I / you / we / they* + V**
***He / she / it* + V + -s** (ou -es pour les verbes se terminant par *-o*, *-ch*, *-sh*, *-s*, *-x* et *-z*).

I always take the train. *Je prends toujours le train.*

He goes to work by bus. *Il va au travail en bus.*

Lorsque le verbe se termine par une consonne et un *-y*, celui-ci se transforme en « i ».

He studies art. *Il étudie l'art.*

Forme négative

Sujet + *don't/doesn't* + V

I don't like fish. *Je n'aime pas le poisson.*

He doesn't smoke. *Il ne fume pas.*

Forme interrogative

***Do/does* + sujet + V + ?**

Do you speak English? *Parles-tu anglais ?*

Does he live in London? *Vit-il à Londres ?*

Construire une question

Mot interrogatif + auxiliaire + sujet + verbe (+ complément) + ?

What do you like best for dinner?
Que préfères-tu pour le dîner ?

Quand le mot interrogatif est sujet :

<u>Who lives</u> at Buckingham Palace?
Qui vit à Buckingham Palace ?

Lire l'heure digitale

On dit les deux nombres l'un après l'autre.

10:30 = ten thirty

11:45 = eleven forty-five

UNIT 2

PROJECT

A2

Create a Survival Kit for a Trip in an English-speaking Country

SCENARIO

Vous allez passer quelques jours en famille d'accueil dans un pays anglophone. Réalisez un kit de survie comprenant le vocabulaire et les phrases utiles pour pouvoir communiquer dans différentes situations.

A1

Lister des mots de vocabulaire et des phrases simples

- Choisissez une situation parmi celles proposées ou trouvez-en une autre.
  - → arrival at the host family's home
  - → transport and directions
  - → food (at the host family's home and at restaurants)
  - → visits
  - → another situation: at the airport, buying souvenirs, shopping, talking about my family, my school and my hobbies with the family...
- Formulez en anglais des phrases-types qui peuvent être utiles à l'étranger.
- Listez pour la situation choisie des mots de vocabulaire utiles.

→ Situation: ....

→ Useful sentences:

....

....

....

....

→ Useful words:

....

....

- Mettez votre travail au propre dans un texteur.
- Illustrez les mots et les phrases types avec des images claires ou traduisez-les.

A2

Enregistrer une liste de mots et de phrases

- Vérifiez la prononciation des mots inconnus dans un dictionnaire en ligne.
- Entraînez-vous à prononcer les phrases et les mots de vocabulaire que vous avez répertoriés dans votre kit de survie.
- Enregistrez-vous et sauvegardez chaque fichier-son sur votre ordinateur.
- Rattachez chaque fichier-son au mot ou à la phrase correspondante (cliquez droit à côté du mot sur votre texteur, puis cliquez sur « insertion », « objet », « créer à partir du fichier »).

Auto évaluation

PORTFOLIO

foucherconnect.fr/21ptt13

UNIT 2

Accompagnement Personnalisé — Prendre part à une conversation

Stratégies

1 Identifiez l'objet de la conversation. Repérez les mots clés.

2 N'ayez pas peur de prendre la parole : restez calme et concentré.

3 Réagissez de façon naturelle, répondez ou donnez votre avis sur le sujet, avec des mots ou des phrases simples. **A** Vous pouvez aussi accompagner vos phrases par des gestes.

4 Soignez votre prononciation. Articulez bien et ne parlez pas trop vite.

5 Utilisez des *gap fillers* si vous hésitez ou si vous cherchez vos mots. **B**

6 Demandez à votre interlocuteur de répéter, de parler moins vite si besoin. **C**

Observation

1 (piste 20) **Écoutez la conversation et complétez.**

a. ………………, guys. Let's start the stadium visit. Do you like football?

b. Yes, of ………………!

c. Me ……………, I'm a big fan of football. ……………, do you know the name of the team playing here at Old Trafford?

d. Er… Could you ……………… that, please?

e. I'm asking if you know the name of the team that plays here at Old Trafford?

f. Oh, OK, I ……………………… . Yes, it is Manchester United. The best team ever!

g. I totally agree with you! And do you know the nickname of the stadium?

h. Er… I know it, but I can't remember. Um… It's … "The Theatre of Dreams"!

i. Great! ……………………!

2 Entourez les *gap fillers* dans le dialogue.

3 Indiquez dans quelle réplique :

a. le locuteur n'a pas compris : ……

b. le locuteur réfléchit : ……

c. le locuteur est d'accord avec son interlocuteur : ……

À vous de jouer !

Discutez des sujets ci-dessous avec votre partenaire. Essayez de parler chacun à votre tour en enchaînant un maximum de répliques.

Sujet 1: Arsenal is the best football team.

Sujet 2: Would you like to live in London? Why?

À retenir

A Pour réagir et donner votre avis	B Les *gap fillers*	C En cas d'incompréhension
– Great! *Super !* – Incredible! *Incroyable !* – Are you joking? *Tu plaisantes ?* – I agree. *Je suis d'accord.* – I don't agree. *Je ne suis pas d'accord.* – I'm not sure. *Je ne suis pas sûr(e).* – Me too/neither. *Moi aussi/non plus.* – Of course! *Bien sûr !*	– Well… *Bon, Eh bien…* – Er…/Um… *Euh…* – Right… *Bon…* – So… *Donc, alors…* – You know… *Tu sais…* – You see… *Tu vois…* – I mean… *Je veux dire…*	– Could you repeat that, please? *Pourriez-vous répéter, s'il vous plaît ?* – Speak up! *Parle plus fort !* – I don't understand. *Je ne comprends pas.* – Can you speak slowly, please? *Pouvez-vous parler lentement ?*

CULTURE CLICK 1 SPACE EXPLORATION

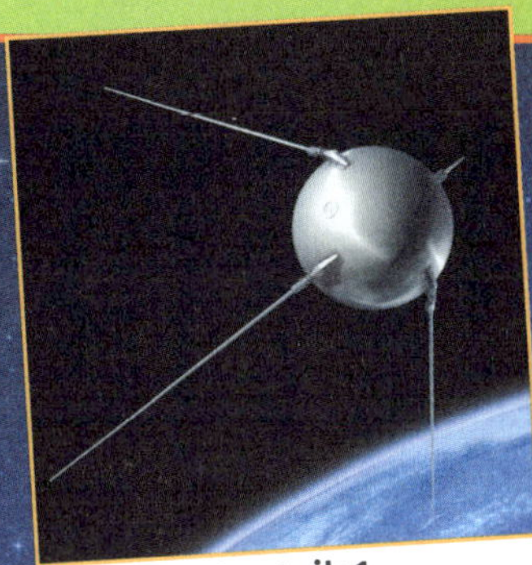

Sputnik 1

....
First artificial satellite

Laika, the space dog

....
First animal in space

Explorer 6

....
First photograph of Earth taken by the NASA

Alexei Leonov

....
First person to walk in space

"That's one small step for man, one giant leap for mankind."

Neil Armstrong

....
First human on the Moon

Sally Ride

....
First American woman in space

Thomas Pesquet

....
First European aboard the SpaceX *Crew Dragon* spacecraft*

* vaisseau spatial

1 21 **Listen and fill in the missing dates.**

2 22 **a. Complete with: *Moon* • *space race* • *United States* • *launched*. Then listen and check.**

The Soviet Union .... *Sputnik 1* on October 4, 1957, before the ...., surprising people all over the world. This major event launched the .... between the Soviet Union and the USA. This space race ended on July 20, 1969, when Neil Armstrong stepped onto the .... for the first time.

b. Explain in French what you have understood.

3 **Choose the correct translation for Neil Armstrong's quotation.**

☐ *C'est un petit pas pour l'humanité, un pas de géant pour l'homme.*
☐ *C'est un petit pas pour l'homme, un pas de géant pour l'humanité.*

QUIZ

1. Cape Canaveral space force station is located in:
- ☐ a. Russia
- ☐ b. the US
- ☐ c. South Africa

2. The first human in space was:
- ☐ a. Neil Armstrong
- ☐ b. Thomas Pesquet
- ☐ c. Yuri Gagarin

3. The Apollo programme was designed to send people to:
- ☐ a. the Moon
- ☐ b. Mars
- ☐ c. Mercury

4. Weightlessness (or zero gravity) causes astronauts to:
- ☐ a. drink a lot
- ☐ b. eat a lot
- ☐ c. float in the air

5. The first female spacewalk was conducted by Jessica Meir and Christina Koch in:
☐ a. 1989 ☐ b. 1999 ☐ c. 2019

6. ISS missions usually last about:
- ☐ a. six months
- ☐ b. three months
- ☐ c. one month

7. NASA is:
- ☐ a. Russian
- ☐ b. Canadian
- ☐ c. American

8. The SpaceX capsule *Endeavour* was launched from:
- ☐ a. New York
- ☐ b. Colorado
- ☐ c. Florida

9. In 2021 NASA's *Perseverance* rover landed on:
☐ a. Saturn ☐ b. Mars ☐ c. Pluto

10. In space, astronauts grow by:
- ☐ a. one to two inches*
- ☐ b. about 6 inches
- ☐ c. about a foot*

**Unités de mesure :* 1 inch = 2,54 cm ; 1 foot = 30,48 cm

23 **Listen and check.**

Your score: ..../10

SpaceX is a privately owned company founded by Elon Musk, the highly revered private space entrepreneur. NASA, on the other hand, is a government-owned and -funded organization. The company launches both commercial and military satellites for its clients. So, that's the difference between SpaceX and NASA.

www.mainenewsonline.com.

Musk founded SpaceX in 2002 (two years before he joined electric car company Tesla) with the goal of eventually building more affordable[1] spacecraft that would make it possible to one day reach and colonize Mars. For approximately $52 million per person, you can purchase a seat to fly with SpaceX to the ISS[2].

www.cnbc.com.

1. *abordable* ; 2. International Space Station

4 Read the documents and answer the questions in French.

a. Quelle est la différence entre la NASA et SpaceX ?

....

....

b. Quel était l'objectif de Musk lorsqu'il a créé SpaceX ?

....

c. Que peut-on acheter pour 52 millions de dollars ?

....

....

5 Watch the video and say what surprizes you most.

Help: freeze-dried food: *de la nourriture lyophilisée* • upside down: *à l'envers, la tête en bas.*

1'40"
VIDÉO
Space Makes Eating a Lot More Fun! Astronauts Explain Food Prep
foucherconnect.fr/21ptt14

UNIT 3

How to Make the Most of an Internship

PROJECT A2+

In order to help fellow pupils on their first internship, you create a tutorial to give them advice.

1 **Look at the picture and say who the people are and what they are doing.**

2 24 **Listen and fill in the definition of an internship with the words below.**

weeks • short-term • employment • pupils • diplomas

An internship is a .... experience of ...., typically arranged by schools for .... Pupils preparing for vocational* .... must do several ....’ internship in a company.

**professionnel*

FLIPPED CLASSROOM

Complete the sentences.

a. A .... or an .... is a person who is learning a job.

b. A .... or a .... is the person who trains a young person for a job.

c. An internship or a .... is the period during which a trainee works.

d. A .... is the place where people work.

e. A .... or a .... is a business in which pupils can do a work placement.

1'30"

CAPSULE
How To Make the Most of an Internship
foucherconnect.fr/21ptt15

UNIT 3

Show Your Personality

ACTIVITY A — Who Are You?

1 (25) **Listen and tick the adjectives corresponding to Mary's personality.**

☐ a. nervous

☐ b. relaxed

☐ c. enthusiastic

☐ d. indifferent

☐ e. shy

☐ f. outgoing

☐ g. punctual

☐ h. late

2 **Say what your two good and bad points are.**

WORD BOX

- **helpful** serviable
- **late** en retard
- **outgoing** ouvert, sociable
- **shake*** **hands** serrer la main
- **well-mannered** bien élevé

ACTIVITY B — Show Your Best Self!

STEP BY STEP → p. 36

1 **Watch the video from 0:45 to 1:13 and tick the correct answers.**

The people in the video advise students to be:

☐ polite ☐ well-mannered ☐ punctual ☐ approachable ☐ helpful
☐ useful ☐ passionate ☐ enthusiastic ☐ interested ☐ confident ☐ efficient

2 **Watch from 1:10 to the end and number the advice given in the video.**

.... Get to know people and socialize.

.... Shake hands well.

.... Make good eye contact.

.... Do the job that other people don't want to do.

.... Do the tasks at the best of your ability.

.... Treat everyone like you're talking to the boss.

.... Learn as much about the job as you possibly can.

2'00"
VIDÉO
How to Make the Best of Work Experience
foucherconnect.fr/21ptt16

3 **Say what you think the three best pieces of advice are.**

ACTIVITY C How to Behave During Your Internship

Code of Ethics for the Student

❶ Be polite and courteous to your employer, fellow workers and clients at all times. [...]

❷ Your appearance and behaviour must be in keeping with the accepted standards of the workplace.

❸ Be punctual in arriving to work and when returning from a break.

❹ Try to show initiative and enthusiasm – ask how you can be of help. [...]

❺ Listen to and carry out carefully all instructions given to you.

❻ Be loyal to your employer. You may be given access to information at work which should NOT be discussed elsewhere. Do not gossip. Do a good job and establish a good reputation.

❼ Make yourself familiar with the safety requirements of the workplace. [...]

Absenteeism

❽ If for any reason you are not able to attend work, you must notify your employer as soon as possible after the start of work that day, and you must notify the school.

Year 10 Work Experience Taster Program,
St Anthony's Catholic College,
24-26th June 2019.

1 Select the correct answer.

a. The document is for: ☐ parents ☐ teachers ☐ students

b. The document gives recommendations for:
☐ the internship ☐ the school

2 Find the English for:

a. *un employeur* (❶): ....

b. *le comportement* (❷): ....

c. *une pause* (❸): ....

d. *dire des ragots* (❻): ....

e. *la sécurité* (❼): ....

f. *aller au travail* (❽): ....

3 Match the synonyms.

a. a tutor •	• 1. a directive
b. a co-worker •	• 2. a difficulty
c. a problem •	• 3. a mentor
d. an instruction •	• 4. a fellow worker
e. requirements •	• 5. necessary conditions

4 Tick "right" or "wrong".

a. You must be polite to everybody in the workplace.
☐ right ☐ wrong

b. You should be late and not follow the instructions.
☐ right ☐ wrong

c. You mustn't gossip. ☐ right ☐ wrong

d. You shouldn't be familiar with the safety requirements.
☐ right ☐ wrong

GRAMMAR SPOT

a. **Be polite.**

b. **Do not gossip.**

➡ *Entourez la forme affirmative.*

➡ *Soulignez la forme négative.*

➡ *Quelle est la construction de la phrase a ?*

....

➡ *Les phrases a et b expriment :*
☐ *une consigne*
☐ *une possibilité*

Training ex. 5 p. 38

WORD BOX

- **carry out** effectuer
- **notify** informer
- **a stain** une tache

ACTION 1

A2+ **Donner des conseils sur l'attitude à adopter en stage**

Give your partner three pieces of advice on how to behave in her/his internship.

UNIT 3

Dress Code and Safety

ACTIVITY D What to Wear

1 26 **Listen and complete the labels.**

2 **Match the English to its French equivalent.**

a. groomed hair •
b. low-heeled shoes •
c. smart trousers •

• 1. *un pantalon habillé*
• 2. *bien coiffé(e)*
• 3. *des chaussures à talons plats*

3 **Orally explain what you must wear during your internship.**

ACTIVITY E What Not to Wear

1 27 **Listen and tick the advice given to Kelly.**

a. You: ☐ shouldn't ☐ should wear dirty clothes.

b. You: ☐ must ☐ mustn't brush your hair properly.

c. You: ☐ should ☐ shouldn't wear clean trousers without holes or a skirt and a better-fitting jumper.

d. Your clothes: ☐ must ☐ mustn't be unkempt* at work.

**négligé*

2 28 **Listen and circle what's happening to Paul.**

a. Paul's boss sent him (*shopping* / *home*).

b. He must change (*his shirt* / *his hairstyle*) because it has (*a stain* / *a hole*).

c. He works (*in a 5-star hotel* / *in a B and B*) (*on the front desk* / *in the restaurant*).

d. He must look (*average* / *perfect*) for the customers.

GRAMMAR SPOT

a. You should brush your hair.
b. You shouldn't wear dirty clothes.
c. You must notify the school.
d. You mustn't be unkempt.

➔ *Soulignez les phrases qui expriment un conseil.*

➔ *Quelle phrase exprime un ordre ?* ....

➔ *Quelle phrase exprime une interdiction ?* ....

➔ *De quoi* should, shouldn't, must *et* mustn't *sont-ils suivis ?*
....

Training ex. 6, 7 & 8 p. 38

ACTION 2 A2+

MÉDIATION

Dire ce que l'on doit porter sur le lieu de travail

29 **Listen to the dialogue and explain to your partner what you have understood.**

ACTIVITY F In Industrial Services

1 Write the numbers corresponding to the equipment in the picture.

In the industrial sector, the most common PPE (Personal Protective Equipment) is the **protective helmet** (.....) or hard hat, **gloves** (.....) for the hands and some type of **boots** (.....) to protect the feet. Most of the jobs require wearing special clothes, **"hi-vis" clothes**[1] (.....) like a vest or trousers. In some specific jobs you must also wear special types of **eye protection** (.....), **ear protection** (.....) and sometimes even a **mask** (.....).

1. high visibility clothes

2 (30) Listen and complete the PPE corresponding to the jobs.

a. **a boilermaker**	b. **a forklift driver**	c. **a fishmonger**
– a helmet with a	– a	– a waterproof PPE: an apron, ..., and gloves
–	– a	– a ....
– an apron	....	

WORD BOX

- **fall*** tomber
- **a folder** un dossier
- **an injury** une blessure
- **prevent** éviter, empêcher
- **stack** empiler
- **trip over** trébucher (sur)

3 (31) Listen and match the PPE with their utility.

a. Helmets •
b. Hi-vis clothes •
c. Gloves •
d. Waterproof clothes •

• 1. prevent hand injuries like burns for instance.
• 2. prevent head injury in case of falling objects.
• 3. help workers be visible in the dark.
• 4. prevent from getting soaked*.

* trempé

ACTIVITY G Safety in the Office

LET'S GO FURTHER!!! →p. 36

1 (32) Listen to Tom and Sarah working for the Health and Safety commission[1] and fill in the blanks.

The office is a .... There are .... and folders stacked in front of doors, so it is extremely .... in case of .... And the office is quite old so the .... needs to be fixed[2]. .... use extension cables[3] and they can trip over them and fall. It is very dangerous.

1. commission hygiène et sécurité; 2. réparé; 3. rallonge électrique

ACTION 3

A2 Écrire des conseils sur la sécurité au travail

Choose a picture p. 119 and write five sentences giving advice.

Differentiated Activities

STEP BY STEP

ACTIVITY B p. 32

1 Watch the video from 0:45 to 1:13 and tick the correct answers.

a. The people are giving advice about: ☐ personal lives ☐ work experience

b. The adjectives mentioned are: ☐ polite ☐ messy ☐ well-mannered ☐ sociable ☐ helpful ☐ confident ☐ stubborn ☐ enthusiastic ☐ interested ☐ punctual ☐ organized

2 Watch from 1:10 to the end and match the beginning of the pieces of advice given with the end.

a. You must shake hands... •
b. Ask your tutor for work... •
c. You should be helpful... •
d. You must do... •

• 1. if you don't have a task to do.
• 2. with your colleagues.
• 3. your best.
• 4. and make good eye contact.

LET'S GO FURTHER!!!

ACTIVITY G p. 35

2'28"
VIDÉO
Health and Safety risk Assessment and Management
foucherconnect.fr/21ptt17

**1 Watch the video from the beginning to 0:23.
Tick True (T) or False (F) and justify your answer when it's false.**

a. Workers must look for things that could cause injuries and illness at work. ☐ T ☐ F

....

b. They must decide if they're taking reasonable steps to encourage injuries. ☐ T ☐ F

....

c. The main goal is to keep people safe and healthy at work. ☐ T ☐ F

....

2 Watch the video from 0:23 to 1:17 and underline the correct answers.

a. Hazards[1] mentioned in the video: (*repeated or heavy lifting – using dangerous tools – using chemicals – badly ventilated room – causes of work-related stress*)

b. Potentially vulnerable people mentioned in the video: (*older people – pregnant workers – babies – young people – people with disabilities*)

1. *dangers*

3 Watch the video from 1:17 to the end and fill in the blanks.

a. Sometimes you might not be able to remove the .... completely. So think about how you can make it less likely to .... harm.

b. For example, you could do the .... another way, use different .... or tools, or provide personal .... equipment.

c. Review what you are doing to .... risk whenever there are significant .... like new staff or equipment.

AUDIO foucherconnect.fr/21ptt18

EXERCICES INTERACTIFS foucherconnect.fr/21ptt19

in TUNE

A 33 **Écoutez les mots ci-dessous et soulignez la syllabe accentuée, puis répétez.**

polite • punctual • organized • messy

B 34 **Soulignez la syllabe accentuée. Écoutez et vérifiez.**

impolite • confident • shy • stubborn • enthusiastic • approachable

1 35 **Remettez les lettres dans l'ordre. Écoutez et vérifiez.**

a. ETAL	b. PILOMIET	c. HYS	d. GONGIOTU ....

2 **Complétez la grille de mots fléchés.**

3 **Reliez chaque adjectif à son opposé.**

a. organized •	• 1. lazy
b. sociable •	• 2. messy
c. punctual •	• 3. shy
d. polite •	• 4. late
e. hard-working •	• 5. impolite

4 **Challenge!**

Listez un maximum de mots liés aux dangers possibles dans votre domaine professionnel.

TRAINING

5 **Transformez les phrases suivantes à l'impératif.**

a. You must be punctual.

....

b. You should work hard.

....

c. You mustn't be impolite.

....

d. You should be well-mannered.

....

e. You mustn't be late.

....

6 **Soulignez le modal qui convient.**

a. In the workplace, you (*should / shouldn't*) be hard-working.
b. You (*mustn't / must*) be punctual.
c. Trainees (*shouldn't / should*) use their mobile phones at work.
d. They (*mustn't / must*) wear PPE outside the company.
e. Interns (*should / shouldn't*) be late.
f. You (*must / mustn't*) wear casual clothes in a very formal workplace.

7 36 **Mettez les éléments suivants dans l'ordre. Écoutez et vérifiez.**

a. to prevent head injury / Construction site workers / a protective helmet / must wear → ....

....

b. for hygiene reasons / must wear / Workers / hats and gloves / in the food industry → ....

....

c. Boilermakers / a helmet with a visor / from the heat / must wear / to protect themselves → ....

....

8 **Observez l'image et écrivez au moins trois phrases pour donner des conseils à cet étudiant qui s'apprête à faire un stage dans un hôtel ou dans un magasin de sport (coiffure, vêtements, chaussures).**
You shouldn't wear... but you should wear...

....

....

....

....

....

....

....

TIPS LANGUAGE

Exprimer une consigne : l'impératif

À la forme affirmative : V (base verbale)

Be polite! *Sois/soyez poli !*

À la forme négative : *do not/don't* + V

Do not gossip! *Ne dis/dites pas de ragots !*

Exprimer un conseil : *should* + V

The trainee should be polite. *Le stagiaire devrait être poli.*

You shouldn't wear dirty clothes. *Tu ne devrais pas porter de vêtements sales.*

Exprimer l'obligation : *must*+ V

You must notify your employer if you're absent. *Vous devez prévenir votre employeur si vous êtes absent.*

Exprimer une interdiction : *mustn't* + V

You mustn't be unkempt. *Vous ne devez pas être négligé.*

UNIT 3

PROJECT

A2+

Create a Tutorial

for Future Interns

SCENARIO

Pour aider des lycéens qui vont débuter leur premier stage, créez un tutoriel pour leur donner des conseils.

A2

Compléter une fiche

- Choisissez un métier qui vous attire ou que vous connaissez.
- Complétez la fiche ci-dessous en rédigeant au moins deux conseils par rubrique.

→ Job: ....

ITEMS

→ Your behaviour

- ....
- ....
- ....
- ....

→ Your dress code including PPE

- ....
- ....
- ....
- ....

→ Your safety

- ....
- ....
- ....
- ....

→ You and your colleagues

- ....
- ....
- ....
- ....

A2+

Réaliser un tuto

- À l'aide de la fiche, répétez votre présentation. Vérifiez la prononciation des mots difficiles dans un dictionnaire.
- Essayez de mettre en scène votre présentation : décor, accessoires…
- Vérifiez votre enregistrement et modifiez-le si besoin.

Auto évaluation

PORTFOLIO

foucherconnect.fr/21ptt20

UNIT 3

Accompagnement personnalisé

Comprendre un document audio ou vidéo

Stratégies

Lors de l'examen du baccalauréat, vous pourrez écouter ou voir le document trois fois.

1 Anticipez le thème du document. Avant la première écoute ou le premier visionnage, utilisez le titre et l'image pour émettre des hypothèses sur le contenu du document (thème, lexique…).

2 Lors de la première écoute, identifiez la nature du document (interview, documentaire, journal télévisé…). Dégagez le thème principal (quel est le sujet ?). Repérez le nombre d'interlocuteurs (combien de personnes parlent ?) et les lieux.

3 Lors de la deuxième écoute, repérez les noms propres, les indications chiffrées et toutes les indications qui vous paraissent importantes.

4 Lors de la troisième écoute, faites le lien entre les différentes informations que vous comprenez et notez les détails.

5 Utilisez vos notes pour synthétiser ce que vous avez compris.

Observation

0'59"
VIDÉO
One-minute World News
foucherconnect.fr/21ptt21

1 Observez le titre et émettez des hypothèses sur le sujet du document.

....

2 Regardez une première fois la vidéo et repérez les éléments ci-dessous :

nature du document – nombre de locuteurs – nombre d'informations présentées

....

3 Regardez une deuxième fois le document et repérez les éléments suivants :

noms propres – pays – indications chiffrées – sujet de chaque reportage

....

....

4 Regardez le document une troisième fois et repérez les détails qui vous avaient échappés.

....

....

À vous de jouer !

1'18"
VIDÉO
5 Proper Workplace Etiquette Tips to Practice for Professional Success
foucherconnect.fr/21ptt22

Faites un résumé du document en suivant les stratégies.

....

....

....

....

UNIT 4 Be Sporty!

PROJECT A2+

Create an interactive quiz about the sport of your choice.

1 **Orally describe the photo.**

2 37 **Listen and tick the right information.**

a. The Paris 2024 Olympics will take place in: ☐ summer ☐ winter

b. On the opening day, ☐ 2,100 ☐ 1,200 American athletes will be present.

c. The logo represents: ☐ a flame burning a medal ☐ Marianne's face looking like a flame

d. It's the: ☐ first ☐ second time that the Olympic and Paralympic Games will have the same logo.

e. The buildings of the Olympic Village will be: ☐ eco-friendly[1] and sustainable[2] ☐ ephemeral

f. There will be breakdance, climbing, skateboarding and: ☐ karate ☐ surfing events

1. écologique, respectueux de l'environnement; 2. durable

FLIPPED CLASSROOM

Complete the sentences.

a. During a world ...., elite sportsmen and women represent their nations.

b. To choose the finalists, the League organises a ....

c. True athletes demonstrate fair play and respect the .... of their sport.

d. Gymnasiums, stadiums and swimming-pools are examples of ....

1'30"
CAPSULE
Be Sporty!
foucherconnect.fr/21ptt23

UNIT 4

Top Level Tournaments

ACTIVITY A Rugby Fans

1 38 Listen and tick the right answer.

a. In: ☐ 1723 ☐ 1823, William Webb Ellis was a pupil at Rugby School in Rugby, England.

b. He created the rugby style of play during a school football match, when he: ☐ picked up the ball and ran with it
☐ scored against his own team

c. Today the Rugby World Cup takes place every: ☐ 2 ☐ 4 ☐ 6 years.

d. A team is made up of: ☐ 7 ☐ 13 ☐ 15 players and a game lasts for 80 minutes.

2 39 Listen to the rules of rugby. Tick Right or Wrong.

	Right	Wrong
a. Players can pass the ball forwards, sideways[1] or backwards.		
b. Players can tackle an opponent in possession of the ball.		
c. The team scores a try when a player puts down the ball behind the goalposts[2].		
d. A team gets points by scoring tries and kicking goals.		

1. de côté; 2. les poteaux

WORD BOX

- **a back** un arrière
- **backward(s)** en arrière
- **a forward** un avant
- **forward(s)** en avant
- **a goal** un but
- **last** durer
- **score** marquer (un but)
- **a try** un essai

ACTIVITY B Sports Teams and Logos

40 Listen to the explanations. Then answer the quiz.

a. The Toronto Rock are a professional Canadian:
☐ soccer team
☐ ice hockey team
☐ lacrosse team

b. The Dallas Cowboys are a football team headquartered in:
☐ Kansas
☐ Texas
☐ Arizona

c. The Australian Diamonds compete against international:
☐ netball teams
☐ volleyball teams
☐ hurling teams

d. In South Africa, cricket is the:
☐ first
☐ second
☐ third
most popular sport.

ACTION 1

Écrire des phrases simples sur le thème du sport A1

Use the information to write a multiple-choice quiz like the one in Activity B.

Name: Manchester United football club; **Nickname:** The Red Devils; **Stadium:** Old Trafford. **Compete in:** Premier League; **Best player:** Fred; **Most recent trophy:** the UEFA Europa League. **Feature***: have won more trophies than any other club in English football.

* *caractéristique*

ACTIVITY C

Qualifying for the World Cup

1 41 **Listen and fill in the information about the event.**

Name of the tournament:

The .... World Cup

Host country: ....

Length: ....

Number of teams: ....

Teams already qualified: ....

....

2 42 **Listen and circle the correct information.**

a. A qualifying event will determine the final (*three* / *eight*) teams that will compete for the World Cup.

b. The 31 matches (*won't* / *will*) be broadcast live.
The event will last (*29* / *39*) days, with the opening match at (*Eden Park in Auckland* / *Seddon Park in Hamilton*).

c. Each team will get ten points for a win, five for a tie[1], no result or abandonment[2] and (*two* / *none*) for a loss.

d. The two winners will meet at the Hagley Oval in Christchurch. They'll play the (*final* / *semi-final*) match in March.

1. *égalité;* 2. *match interrompu ou annulé*

GRAMMAR SPOT

a. The event will take place next year. They'll play the final match.

b. The women's Cricket World Cup won't take place this year.

c. Will the Paralympic Games happen next year?

➔ *Soulignez l'auxiliaire dans chaque énoncé.*

➔ *Le temps employé est le :*
☐ *prétérit* ☐ *présent* ☐ *futur*

➔ *Observez les phrases* **a** *et* **b** *et complétez :*
will / 'll / won't + ...

Training ex. 4 & 5 page 48

ACTIVITY D

Sporting Events Around the World

Use the elements to answer the questions orally and present the news.

a. Will the Paralympic Games happen next year?

b. Will the World Beach Games soon resume*?

c. When will the badminton World Championships begin?

d. Where will the World Athletics Championships take place?

* *reprendre*

ACTION 2

A2 **Donner des explications sur des projets futurs**

Choose one of the events and describe what will happen.

INTERNET
foucherconnect.fr/21ptt24

Sports for Life

ACTIVITY E A Top Prospect

LET'S GO FURTHER !!! →p. 46

The two American professional baseball players in the photo are Joey Bart and Hunter Pence. They play with the San Francisco Giants team. Here, Joey Bart is in the catcher's position. He is waiting to catch the ball in his mitt. He is wearing a chest protector and leg guards. As you can see, Hunter Pence is wearing gloves to hold his bat. He is preparing to hit the ball. His sliding* shorts will protect him. They are both wearing helmets and baseball cleats.

*de glisse

Read the text. Write the underlined words on the right label.

WORD BOX

- **able-bodied** valide
- **cleats (US)** chaussures à crampons
- **disability** le handicap
- **inability** l'incapacité
- **a wheelchair** un fauteuil roulant

ACTIVITY F Disabled but not Unable

1 Watch the whole video and write the sports you hear.

....

2 Watch again and underline the correct information.

a. Alicia Guerrero is (*15* / *16* / *18*).

b. She has been playing wheelchair basketball for (*a year* / *two years* / *three years*).

c. Parasport is just as (*easy* / *difficult* / *competitive*) as able-bodied basketball.

d. Her disability gives her the (*courage* / *strength* / *power*) to continue. Disability is not inability.

0'53"
VIDÉO
Disability is not inability: Alicia's Story | Guardian
foucherconnect.fr/21ptt25

ACTIVITY G

Sustainable Stadiums

STEP BY STEP →p. 46

New report reaffirms Qatar 2022's commitment to sustainability

Modular design means more than 170,000 seats can be donated

The FIFA World Cup™ demands increased[1] seating capacity compared to Qatar's local needs – and the solution to this challenge is modular stadiums. More than 170,000 stadium seats will be removed from several venues after the tournament, with the SC[2] planning to donate them to countries which lack sporting infrastructure [...]. Thanks to the modular design, it will be easy to disassemble facilities, transport them to a new location and reuse them. [...]

Stadiums will be operational year-round

Retractable roofs and advanced, energy-efficient cooling technology mean the stadiums can be used year-round. After the tournament, parts of some stadiums will be repurposed into community facilities such as hospitals, schools, retail units and hotels.

www.fifa.com, 9th September 2020.

1. *accrue;* 2. Supreme Committee

1 Read the text and underline the right answer.

The text is about: finding seats for a stadium / greeting football teams / recycling stadiums / playing football matches

2 Find the English for:

a. *un défi* (§1): ....

b. *retirés de plusieurs lieux* (§1): ....

c. *manquer de* (§1): ....

d. *à faible consommation d'énergie* (§2): ....

e. *une technologie de climatisation* (§2): ....

3 Answer the questions.

a. What will happen to the 170,000 stadium seats after the event?

....

....

b. Why will it be easy to disassemble the different parts of the stadium?

....

c. How will the stadiums be used by the community?

....

....

GRAMMAR SPOT

a. He is preparing to hit the ball.

b. They are wearing a helmet.

→ *Le présent en -ing s'utilise lorsqu'une action :*

☐ *est habituelle*

☐ *se passe au moment où l'on parle*

→ *L'auxiliaire du présent en -ing est* ....

→ *Le verbe conjugué se termine par* ....

Training ex. 6 & 7 page 48

ACTION 3

A1

Écrire des phrases sur des actions en cours

Use the pictures online. Write a true or a false statement about each of them to describe the action which is taking place. Submit your sentences to your partner who must decide whether they are true or false.

WWW INTERNET foucherconnect.fr/21ptt26

Differentiated Activities

LET'S GO FURTHER!!! ACTIVITY E

p. 44

VIDÉO
Who's That Kid? Joey Bart
foucherconnect.fr/21ptt27
2'41"

1 Watch the whole video and fill in the information.

a. The word Joey Bart repeats throughout the video is: ....

b. The name of his new team is: ....

2 Watch from 1:00 to the end. Tick the right option to answer the questions.

a. How many games did he play? ☐ 5 games ☐ 10 games ☐ 12 games
b. Did he hit the ball? ☐ Yes, he hit it hard. ☐ No, he missed the ball. ☐ No, he didn't respond.
c. How did he feel when he had to walk away from the game? ☐ Very angry ☐ Very upset ☐ Very happy
d. How long did he stay away from the team? ☐ Seven weeks ☐ Seventeen weeks ☐ Seventy weeks
e. What is his ultimate goal? Making: ☐ an impact ☐ an impression ☐ a presence felt at the highest level of the game.

STEP BY STEP ACTIVITY G

p. 45

1 Read the text and tick the right answer.

The text is about: ☐ finding seats for a stadium ☐ recycling stadiums ☐ playing football matches

2 Match the French words and their translations.

a. *un défi* (§1) •	• 1. removed from several venues
b. *retirés de plusieurs lieux* (§1) •	• 2. lack
c. *manquer de* (§1) •	• 3. a challenge
d. *la conception modulaire* (§1) •	• 4. cooling technology
e. *à faible consommation d'énergie* (§2) •	• 5. the modular design
f. *une technologie de climatisation* (§2) •	• 6. energy-efficient

3 Tick Right or Wrong. Underline the elements in the text to justify your answers.

	Right	Wrong
a. Qatar will design modular stadiums.		
b. Qatar will sell the stadium seats to countries with poor infrastructure.		
c. It will be easy to remove and reuse the facilities.		
d. The stadium can't be used in summer.		
e. The stadium will become a hospital.		

Training

AUDIO foucherconnect.fr/21ptt28

EXERCICES INTERACTIFS foucherconnect.fr/21ptt29

in TUNE

A 43 **Écoutez la prononciation de la lettre « u » dans les mots suivants. Répétez-les.**

club /ʌ/ union /juː/ blue /uː/ put /ʊ/ pressure /ʃə/

B 44 **Classez les mots selon la prononciation de la lettre « u ». Écoutez et vérifiez puis répétez-les.**

rugby • reproduce • rules • result • values • united • feature • full

club /ʌ/	union /juː/	blue /uː/	put /ʊ/	pressure /ʃə/
....	....	....	....	....
....	....	....	....	....
....	....	....	....	....

1 45 **Complétez le nom de ces équipements. Écoutez et vérifiez.**

a. a	b. a	c. a	d.	e. ....

2 **Complétez la grille à l'aide des illustrations.**

Challenge!

3 Vous avez 2 minutes pour associer 5 sports à des sportifs célèbres, aux équipements qui leur sont indispensables, et aux lieux où ils sont pratiqués.

Training

4 (46) Écoutez et complétez les énoncés.

a. ...., I will meet my friends at the sports hall.

b. ...., the matches will resume.

c. The students will need their sports gear*
....

d. The champions will show fair play in
................................'s competition.

*affaires de sport

5 Réécrivez les énoncés suivants au futur.

a. I play badminton at the gymnasium.

....

....

b. We don't go and see the match.

....

c. Do you watch the Super Bowl on TV?

....

d. There is an autograph on this ball.

....

....

6 Conjuguez les verbes entre parenthèses au présent en *-ing*.

a. He is at the stadium. He .... for the competition. (practise)

b. .... they .... in the woods in this heavy rain? (run)

c. We .... the real game because we have adapted the rules. (not play)

d. I am at the station. I .... for the bus. (wait)

7 Écrivez un énoncé pour décrire ce que les personnages sont en train de faire sur ces photos.

a. ride
....

b. ski
....

c. run
....

d. jump
....

TIPS — LANGUAGE

Le futur

Il s'utilise pour parler d'une action ou d'un événement qui va se dérouler dans l'avenir.

***will* + V / *'ll* + V**

The teams will qualify through varied test matches. *Les équipes se qualifieront lors d'épreuves variées.*

(When) will the tournament take place? *(Quand) le tournoi aura-t-il lieu ?*

***will not* + V / *won't* + V**

Due to a recent injury, this football player won't play until next spring. *À cause d'une blessure récente, ce footballer ne jouera pas avant le printemps prochain.*

Le présent en *-ing*

Il s'utilise pour décrire une action en cours au moment où l'on parle.

be* au présent + V *-ing

Where are you going? I am going to the swimming-pool. *Où vas-tu ? Je vais à la piscine.*

The champion is preparing to break the world record. *Le champion se prépare à battre le record du monde.*

The competitions which are taking place at the moment host many athletes. *Les compétitions qui se déroulent en ce moment accueillent de nombreux athlètes.*

UNIT 4 PROJECT A2+

Create an Interactive Quiz about Sport

SCENARIO

Créez un quiz interactif pour promouvoir le sport de votre choix.

A2

Trouver des informations sur un sport

- Choisissez un sport que vous aimez ou que vous pratiquez.
- Cherchez des informations spécifiques à ce sport (type de sport, lieux, équipes, joueurs, règles, équipement, etc.) pour compléter chaque catégorie de la fiche.
- Sélectionnez une image décrivant ce sport et un logo s'il en existe un. Rédigez une courte légende pour décrire cette image et ce logo.

→ The sport of my choice: ....

→ Photos and logos
Picture 1 – description: ....
....
Logo – description: ....
....

→ Type of sport
☐ Individual
☐ Team sport
☐ Indoor sport
☐ Outdoor sport

→ General information
Number of players: ....
Place to practise: ....
....
....

→ Famous sports men and women or teams
....

→ Famous places
....
....

→ Famous events
....
....

→ Specific gear* and equipment
....
....

→ Rules
....
....

→ Future events
....
....

* *affaires de sport*

A2+

Réaliser un quiz sur un sport

- Donnez un titre à votre quiz en spécifiant le sport concerné.
- Pour chaque catégorie de la fiche, rédigez un énoncé et proposez trois solutions possibles dont l'une est la bonne réponse.
- De la même façon, pour l'image et le logo que vous avez sélectionnés, proposez trois descriptions dont une seule est correcte.

Voici un exemple du type de questionnaire que vous pourriez imaginer :

→ 1. The best player is:
a. Cristiano Ronaldo ☐
b. Michael Jordan ☐
c. David Beckham ☐

→ 2. In the photo, the player:
a. is jumping ☐
b. is swimming ☐
c. is running ☐

→ 3. You can:
a. kick the ball ☐
b. hold the ball in your hand ☐
c. catch the ball in your arms ☐

- Imprimez votre quiz ou déposez-le sur un site en ligne pour le soumettre à vos camarades.

Auto évaluation

PORTFOLIO

foucherconnect.fr/21ptt30

Accompagnement Personnalisé Comprendre un document écrit

Stratégies

1 **Observez les éléments du paratexte** (titre, illustrations, source, date, sous-titres, mots en gras, etc.) pour **émettre des hypothèses** sur le contenu.

2 **Lisez le texte dans sa totalité** pour **vérifier les hypothèses émises, définir le type de texte** (descriptif, argumentatif, etc.) et en **dégager le thème principal.**

3 **Lisez à nouveau** le texte **paragraphe par paragraphe** pour définir **les idées principales**, repérer **les étapes** (chronologie, mots de liaison) et affiner **votre compréhension** (contexte, mots connus).

4 **Reliez les informations entre elles** pour faire sens et reconstituer **l'essentiel du texte.**

Observation

Tiger Woods will not be part of the 'Match III' charity event when it tees up[3] on Friday November 27, according to a report in Sportico.

Tiger Woods will not take part in 'the Match III', but Phil Mickelson will

'The Match' is a charity golf event that Turner Sports first introduced between Woods and Phil Mickelson in 2018, a match that was eventually won by Mickelson in a playoff[1] where he scooped[2] the $10 million prize. [...]

According to an article in Sportico this week, Mickelson and Manning will return for 'The Match III', but Woods and Brady will bypass the exhibition match that Thanksgiving Weekend.

Andy Roberts, www.golfmagic.com, Fri, 16 Oct 2020.

1. le match décisif; 2. remporter; 3. démarrer la partie en plaçant une balle sur le tee

1 **Observez le document ci-dessus. Écrivez vos observations et vos hypothèses de lecture.**

Observation	Hypothèses
Type de document et date de parution:	Thème général du document: ....
Titre:	Type de nouvelle développée: ....
Illustration:	....

2 **Surlignez les noms propres, les dates et les indications chiffrées puis résumez l'idée principale de chaque paragraphe par une phrase en français.**

....

....

À vous de jouer !

Lisez le document intitulé *Why Ethics in Sports is Important* et faites-en un compte rendu en français.

www INTERNET

foucherconnect.fr/21ptt31

CULTURE CLICK 2 THE FBI

1 47 **Observe the picture and fill in the labels with the words below. Listen and check.**

courtroom testimonies[1] • paperwork • training • victims, witnesses[2] and suspects • various crimes

1. *des témoignages*; 2. *des témoins*

2 48 **Listen and complete with the following words:**

world • security • justice • protect • corruption • Investigation • crime • terrorism

a. The Federal Bureau of ...., or FBI, is a national .... organization.

b. The FBI's mission is to .... the USA and maintain ....

c. It investigates .... across the country.

d. It protects the United States from ...., espionage, crime, and public ....

e. Today, it is considered one of the ....'s best security and crime-fighting forces.

3 49 **Listen and circle the correct answer.**

To become a special agent, you must:

a. be a (*UK / US*) citizen.

b. be between (*23 and 36 / 33 and 46*) years of age.

c. have a valid (*driver's / firearms*) license.

d. have (*a bachelor's degree / no degree*).

e. be (*tall and strong / physically fit*).

f. have (*two / ten*) years of professional work experience.

QUIZ

1. The creator of the FBI was:
- ☐ a. Charles Joseph Bonaparte
- ☐ b. Abraham Lincoln
- ☐ c. George Washington

2. The FBI was created in:
☐ a. 1880 ☐ b. 1908 ☐ c. 1948

3. The motto* of the FBI is:
- ☐ a. Files, Badges, Investigations
- ☐ b. Force, Behaviour, Intelligence
- ☐ c. Fidelity, Bravery, Integrity

4. The FBI employs about:
- ☐ a. 35,000 people
- ☐ b. 45,000 people
- ☐ c. 55,000 people

5. The FBI headquarters are in:
- ☐ a. Los Angeles
- ☐ b. New York
- ☐ c. Washington DC

6. The FBI training facility is in:
- ☐ a. Portland, Oregon
- ☐ b. San Francisco, California
- ☐ c. Quantico, Virginia

7. FBI agents who die on duty are remembered thanks to:
- ☐ a. the Wall of Honor
- ☐ b. the Wall of Heroes
- ☐ c. the Wall of Memories

8. J. Edgar Hoover was the director of the FBI for:
- ☐ a. 18 years
- ☐ b. 48 years
- ☐ c. 68 years

9. The "Ten Most Wanted Fugitives" list was created in:
☐ a. 1910 ☐ b. 1950 ☐ c. 1980

10. The series that presents the beginning of criminal profiling is:
- ☐ a. *The Mentalist*
- ☐ b. *Mindhunter*
- ☐ c. *Criminal Minds*

* *la devise*

52 **Listen and check.**

Your score: ..../10

4 50 **Listen to the first part of the document and circle the correct answers.**

a. The FBI Youth Leadership Program takes place every (*summer / winter*) in (*Quantico / Orlando*).
b. The participants are (*12-14 / 14-16*) years old and they come from (*America / across the globe*).
c. It lasts (*8 / 10*) days and it is (*free / expensive*).
d. The objective is to learn about (*the FBI / the system of criminal justice / the police / criminal courts*).
e. The program consists of (*classroom study / physical challenges*).

5 51 **Listen to the second part of the document and fill in the blanks.**

"We try to develop .... that they have, and we take them out of their comfort zone and force them to take a look at .... and who they ...., and recognize that they can accomplish ...."

It has been called [...] the capital of the world, but no one has ever been victimized there. This town isn't listed on any official map[1], but it is visited nearly every day and appears often in the movies and on television.

Hogan's Alley is no ordinary place. It's a mock[2] town where new FBI agents and their law enforcement partners learn the ropes through a series of realistic and often stressful scenarios. Whether investigating criminal and terrorist activities, gathering intelligence, processing evidence[3], getting into simulated gunfights, or making arrests, agents and other trainees are taught the latest techniques and challenged to make the right decisions – with the help of actors playing criminals, victims and bystanders.

www.fbi.gov.

1. *une carte géographique* ; 2. *fausse, simulée* ; 3. *des preuves*

6 **Read the document and say in French what you have understood.**

UNIT 5 Essential Workers Needed

PROJECT A2+

Your school wants to list information online about possible careers to help students make a choice. Create and post a job description for this site.

1 **Observe the document and orally explain what it is about.**

2 53 **Use the vocabulary to complete the sentences. Then listen and check.**

delivery people • working people • community • teachers • doctors • police officers

a. Many .... are on the front lines[1] to help their .... They deserve[2] our public thanks and support.

b. Essential workers are .... who treat[3] us and .... who educate us.

c. They are also .... who protect us and .... who bring food or other products to our homes.

1. en première ligne; 2. mériter; 3. soigner

Find the synonyms.

a. a charge, a mission: ....

b. an employee: ....

c. crucial, vital, necessary: ....

d. useful, friendly: ....

e. with a good salary: ....

1'30"
CAPSULE
Essential Workers Needed
foucherconnect.fr/21ptt32

UNIT 5

Frontline Jobs

ACTIVITY A Job Overview

1 Match the jobs and the corresponding tasks.

a. nursing assistant 

b. electrician 

c. supermarket cashier 

d. bus driver 

1. You install, maintain and repair electrical power, communications, lighting. You control systems in homes, businesses and factories.
2. You look after patients in hospitals or you help patients in their own homes. You work with doctors and nurses.
3. You transport passengers from one place to another. You are responsible for their safety and comfort.
4. You scan products and collect payment. You are courteous and helpful with customers.

2 Find the English for:

a. *le courant électrique* (1): ....

b. *l'éclairage* (1): ....

c. *encaisser les paiements* (4): ....

d. *serviable* (4): ....

WORD BOX

- **the community** la collectivité, la société
- **healthy** sain
- **look after** s'occuper de
- **provide** fournir
- **safety** la sécurité
- **welfare** le bien-être

ACTIVITY B Amelia, the Food Producer

54 **Listen and circle the information you hear.**

Job title	(*market / vegetable*) gardener
Main tasks	She (*plants / grows*), cultivates and harvests[1] (*vegetables / fruit*).
Other tasks	She (*sends / sells*) her products at the local (*market / supermarket*). She also provides vegetables to (*groceries / restaurants*).
Role in the community	Thanks to her, people can eat (*healthy / organic*) vegetables grown near their homes.

1. *récolter*

ACTION 1

STEP BY STEP →p. 58

A2 **Rédiger un paragraphe donnant un aperçu d'un métier**

Choose a job in the list below and write a short job description.

Taxi driver / Old-age carer / Fruit producer / Plumber

Help! a carer: *un personnel soignant* • old people's homes: *maisons de retraite* • pipes: *tuyaux*

ACTIVITY C Working in a Warehouse[1]

55 Match the questions to the corresponding answers. Then listen and check.

a. What do you do? •	• 1. I work in a large warehouse.
b. Where do you work? •	• 2. I prepare orders and pack them into boxes.
c. What company do you work for? •	• 3. I am a warehouse assistant.
d. What does your job consist of? •	• 4. I work for Decathlon.
e. Why is your job essential? •	• 5. Because thanks to us, people who can't go shopping can receive their orders at home.

1. *un entrepôt*

ACTIVITY D More Information about Essential Jobs

1 56 **Fill in using the elements below. Then listen and check.**

recycling • waste collector • people • streets • helps • collects (*ramasse*) • organises • childcare worker • looks after • safety

a

Job title: ....
Place of work: in Manchester ....
or in a .... centre
Company: Manchester City Council
Main function: He .... waste and recyclables.
Role in the community: He has a vital role because he .... protect .... from health and environmental problems.

b

Job title: ....
Place of work: Childcare Centre
Company: Western Daycare
Main function: She .... children.
She .... activities and games for them.
Role in the community: She ensures[2] their .... and welfare.

GRAMMAR SPOT

a. **I am a warehouse assistant.**
b. **He is an electrician.**
c. **She sells vegetables.**

➜ *Pour indiquer son métier, on utilise :* ☐ **be** + *nom de métier* ☐ **be** + **a/an** + *nom de métier*

➜ *On emploie le déterminant :* ☐ a ☐ an *devant un mot commençant par un son voyelle.*

➜ *L'article indéfini « des » n'existe pas en anglais.* ☐ *Vrai* ☐ *Faux*

Training ex. 6 & 7 p. 60

2. *assurer*

2 **Work in pairs. You are Max or Liz: ask and answer questions about each other's job.**

ACTION 2

Comprendre des informations sur un métier A2

57 **Listen and write the information about Ryan's job in French.**

Job	....
Main tasks	....
Other tasks	....
Role in the community	....

Jobs That Serve the Community

ACTIVITY E

Job Description

Ambulance care assistant

Ambulance care assistants take patients to and from hospital for appointments.

Average salary (a year)
£19,737 Starter → £21,142 Experienced

Typical hours
43 to 45 a week

You could work
evenings / weekends / bank holidays on shifts

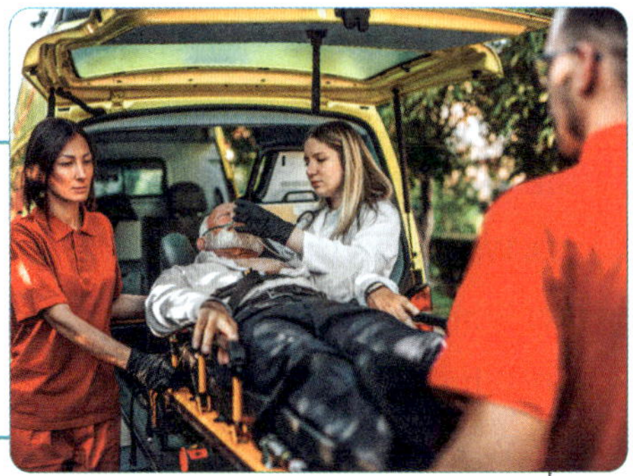

How to become an ambulance care assistant

→ **Entry Requirements**[1]**:** You'll usually need 5 GCSEs[2] [...].

→ **Skills and Knowledge:** You'll need: sensitivity and understanding, patience and the ability to remain calm in stressful situations [...], to be able to carry out basic tasks on a computer or hand-held device[3].

→ **Restrictions and requirements:** You'll need to have a full driving licence [...], have a good level of fitness.

→ **Day-to-day tasks:** You may: help patients out of their home and into the ambulance (it may involve lifting[4]), settle patients back at home after their appointments, use a radio to keep in touch with the ambulance control room, check and maintain the ambulance and its equipment, keep accurate records of journeys[5].

https://nationalcareers.service.gov.uk.

1. *conditions;* 2. *équivalent du brevet des collèges;* 3. *un appareil portable;* 4. *porter, soulever;* 5. *comptes rendus précis des trajets*

1 **Look at the title and subtitle and say what you think the document is about.**

2 **Read the article. Say if the statements are right or wrong and justify.**

a. You don't need any diplomas to become an ambulance care assistant.

....

b. For this job, you don't need to be in good physical condition.

....

3 **Find the English for:**

a. *des rendez-vous* (intro): ....

b. *salaire moyen* (schéma): ....

c. *compétences et connaissances* (§2): ....

d. *un permis de conduire valide* (§3): ....

4 **Answer the questions.**

a. What are the three main personal qualities you need for the job?

....

....

b. What are the technical skills you need for the job?

....

....

c. What can be the advantages and the difficulties of the job?

....

....

GRAMMAR SPOT

a. It may involve lifting.
b. You may help patients.
c. Shari can drive the truck.

→ *Soulignez les verbes modaux qui indiquent l'éventualité.*

→ *Entourez le verbe modal qui indique la capacité.*

→ *Ils se construisent:*
☐ *Sujet + modal + V*
☐ *Sujet + modal + V-ing*

Training ex. 8, 9 & 10 p. 60

ACTIVITY F Be a Firefighter

LET'S GO FURTHER!!! → p. 58

1 Watch the video and number the different parts in the order you see them.

...... What Shari does every morning.

...... What she learnt at college.

...... Introducing herself.

...... Reasons why she applied to be a firefighter.

...... Her top three tips to become a firefighter.

...... What she likes about her job.

2'49"
VIDÉO
Get my job / Be a firefighter
foucherconnect.fr/21ptt33

2 Watch the video from 2:00 to 2:16. Complete what Shari says.

"So, the things I like about my job is working with ...., working within .... and getting to learn something .... every day; but, most of all, being out in the community to .... in the worst days of their lives and putting life first."

3 Watch the video from 2:16 to 2:49. Tick what she says.

a. Apply yourself in school to be great at: ☐ mathematics ☐ physics

b. Apply yourself in sports to develop your: ☐ leadership ☐ teamwork skills
and your physical: ☐ address ☐ fitness

c. Learn how to be safe. Thank you for joining us. We'll see you soon. Keep: ☐ safe ☐ cool

ACTIVITY G What They Think about Their Jobs

WORD BOX
- **apply yourself** s'appliquer
- **get* on well** bien s'entendre
- **motivating** motivant
- **rewarding** gratifiant

1 (58) Listen and circle what Emily says.

a. **Job title:** I am a supermarket (*worker / cashier*).

b. **Difficulties:** I have (*long / hard*) days and I am not very (*well dressed / well paid*).

c. **Positive aspects:** I get on well with my co-workers, who are very (*nice / friendly*). I meet many different people and it is always (*motivating / rewarding*) when you can help people.

d. **Role in the community:** I know my role is very (*useful / helpful*) to the community because people need to (*have / buy*) goods every day.

2 (59) Fill in what Liam thinks about his job with the words below. Then listen and check.

safe • worker • rewarding • team • essential • outdoors

I am a construction .... I like my job but working .... can be difficult when it's hot or rainy. However, working in a good .... is very motivating: we always support each other. And it is very .... because our role is .... to help build quality homes where families can be .... and happy.

ACTION 3 A2+

Donner un avis sur un métier

Write a short paragraph to give your opinion about one of the jobs mentioned in activities E, F or G.

Differentiated Activities

STEP BY STEP

ACTION 1

p. 54

1 Complete this short job description for a taxi driver using the words below.

collect • drive • responsible • service (*assurer l'entretien de*)

Taxi drivers .... passengers from one place to another in their taxis. They are .... for the safety and comfort of their clients. They .... payments. They clean and .... their taxis.

2 Use the vocabulary below to write a short job description for old-age carers.

look after • elderly people (*personnes agées*) • old people's homes (*maisons de retraite*) • help • own homes • doctors and nurses

....

....

....

....

LET'S GO FURTHER!!!

ACTIVITY E

p. 57

1 Watch the video from the beginning to 0:50. Tick True or False and justify.

a. Shari's father was a firefighter and she wanted to be just like him. ☐ True ☐ False

....

b. She was working as a crane operator[1] when she applied to be a firefighter. ☐ True ☐ False

....

1. *grutier*

2 Watch the video from 0:50 to 1:05 and complete.

I went through .... rounds of Internet testing and then passed a physical, through to .... We then went to college for .... weeks before I came out and started my time at the City of Sydney fire ....

3 Watch the video from 1:05 to 2:00 and tick the correct answers.

a. At college, Shari learnt how to respond in case of: ☐ minor vehicle rescue ☐ vehicle extrication ☐ urban fire ☐ forest fire ☐ wildfire ☐ high-rise fire ☐ electrical fire ☐ kitchen fire

b. At college, she also learnt how to: ☐ drive ☐ repair the trucks. She had to: ☐ go out of the truck ☐ take the truck out and go around a: race ☐ tour ☐ course

c. She has to know a lot of: ☐ places ☐ roads so they can get there as: ☐ swift ☐ quick as possible.

Training

AUDIO foucherconnect.fr/21ptt34

EXERCICES INTERACTIFS foucherconnect.fr/21ptt35

in TUNE

A 60 **Écoutez et répétez les mots suivants.** /æ/ have /eɪ/ place /ɑː/ large /ɔː/ walk

B 61 **Classez les mots ci-dessous en fonction de la prononciation de la lettre « a ». Puis écoutez et vérifiez.**

cashier • market • patient • rewarding • task • ambulance • take • install

/æ/	/eɪ/	/ɑː/	/ɔː/
....	....	....	....
....	....	....	....

1 **Associez chaque métier au secteur d'activité correspondant.**

a. supermarket worker •
b. doctor •
c. warehouse assistant •
d. ambulance care assistant •
e. waste collector •
f. farm worker •

• 1. healthcare
• 2. sales
• 3. transport
• 4. agriculture
• 5. delivery and storage
• 6. environment

2 62 **Notez les noms de métier correspondant aux images. Puis écoutez et vérifiez.**

a. ....

b. ....

c. ....

d. ....

e. ....

3 **Complétez les phrases à l'aide des mots ci-dessous.**

repair • collect • install • cultivate • deliver • look after

a. Supermarket cashiers .... payment.
b. Childcare workers .... children.
c. Mechanics .... cars and motorbikes.
d. Farmers .... and harvest cereals, vegetables and fruit.
e. When you order food on line, people .... it to your home.
f. Plumbers .... water pipes.

4 **Retrouvez l'adjectif correspondant à la définition donnée.**

a. Giving or ready to give help: ....
b. Giving a reward, making you satisfied: ....
c. Earning or providing a good salary: ....
d. In a good physical and mental condition: ....
e. Absolutely necessary: ....

Challenge!

5 **Vous avez 2 minutes pour trouver le plus grand nombre possible de mots en lien avec un des métiers de l'exercice 3.**

6 **Soulignez l'article qui convient.**

a. (*a* / *an*) rewarding mission
b. (*a* / *an*) essential role
c. (*a* / *an*) helpful colleague
d. (*a* / *Ø*) good teams
e. (*Ø* / *an*) old-age carer

7 **Ajoutez l'article indéfini si nécessaire.**

a. Mary is ...... student. She wants to be ...... apple producer.
b. Rick and Kate are ...... nursing assistants. They work in ...... hospital.
c. Greg had ...... internship in ...... garage. He would like to be ...... mechanic.
d. I worked with ...... helpful colleagues who encouraged me to start ...... apprenticeship.
e. Delivery people are ...... essential workers. They often have ...... long working days.

8 **Encadrez le verbe modal qui convient.**

a. Many tourist guides (*can* / *can't*) speak English.
b. Bus drivers (*may* / *may not*) smoke during their service.
c. Waste collectors (*may* / *may not*) work in a recycling centre.
d. Supermarket cashiers (*can* / *can't*) be impolite to customers.

9 63 **Écoutez et complétez. Puis soulignez les modaux qui indiquent la capacité et entourez ceux qui indiquent l'éventualité ou la permission.**

a. My neighbour is a very helpful teenager. She .... delicious food.
b. She .... my computer but she .... my bike.
c. She .... me do my homework but I .... her with her studies.
d. I .... her next year because she .... in another town.

10 **Traduisez les énoncés suivants.**

a. Il est possible que le taxi soit en retard.

....

....

b. Il ne sait pas conduire un bus.

....

....

c. Ils ne sont pas autorisés à quitter le travail.

....

....

TIPS LANGUAGE

L'article indéfini *a* / *an* / *Ø*

Emploi

Au singulier (un, une), on emploie *a* devant un son consonne et *an* devant un son voyelle.

a secretary, a uniform *une secrétaire, un uniforme*

an assistant, an hour *un assistant, une heure*

Au pluriel (des), il n'y a pas d'article (Ø).

Ø jobs, Ø cars, Ø people *des emplois, des voitures, des gens.*

Indiquer son métier : S + be + *a*/*an* + métier

She is a singer. *Elle est chanteuse.*

He is an electrician. *Il est électricien.*

Les verbes modaux *can* et *may*

Les modaux sont toujours suivis d'une base verbale (infinitif sans *to*).

- *Can* et *may* peuvent indiquer tous deux la permission.
- *May* indique souvent l'éventualité.
- Seul *can* peut indiquer la capacité.

You may not/can't leave now. *Tu ne peux pas/n'es pas autorisé à partir maintenant.*

She may come. *Il est possible qu'elle vienne.*

I can swim. I can't drive. *Je peux/sais nager. Je ne peux/sais pas conduire.*

UNIT 5

PROJECT

A2+

Post a Job Description

SCENARIO

Dans le cadre du parcours Avenir, votre établissement souhaite mettre en ligne des fiches métiers. Vous devez rédiger et publier une de ces fiches.

A2

Trouver les informations pertinentes sur un métier

- Choisissez un métier qui vous intéresse ou que vous connaissez.
- Trouvez les informations utiles pour compléter la fiche ci-dessous.

→ Job title: ....

Main tasks: ....
....
Average salary: ....
Typical hours: ....
Qualifications: ....
....
Skills and knowledge: ....
....
Restrictions and requirements: ....
....
Day-to-day tasks:
....
....
....
....
....
Role in the community: ....
....
....
Advantages and difficulties of the job: ....
....
....
....

A2+

Réaliser une fiche métier

- Rédigez votre fiche métier à l'aide des informations trouvées. Si besoin, vous pouvez y ajouter d'autres précisions utiles.
- Insérez une ou deux illustrations.
- Relisez bien votre fiche métier et mettez-la en ligne.

Auto évaluation

PORTFOLIO

foucherconnect.fr/21ptt36

UNIT 5

Accompagnement Personnalisé — Interagir à l'écrit

Stratégies

1 Analysez le sujet en tenant compte de la situation d'énonciation:
- qui parle?
- à qui?
- où et quand?

2 Faites un plan pour lister et organiser vos idées. Vous pouvez chercher du vocabulaire dans un dictionnaire ou dans votre manuel.

3 Rédigez votre écrit au brouillon. Respectez les consignes (nombre de mots, codes de mise en forme pour email, carte postale…). Faites des phrases simples. Utilisez des connecteurs pour lier vos idées. **A**

4 Finalisez votre écrit. Corrigez et améliorez votre écrit. Mettez-le au propre.

Observation

1 Lisez le haut du document (question et début de réponse) et indiquez:

a. Le sujet en discussion sur le site Quora:

....

b. Les informations sur les deux internautes:

....

2 Lisez tout le document et entourez les connecteurs. Puis, notez les intentions de l'auteur (A, B, C ou D) à côté de la partie du message correspondant.

A: conclure – **B:** parler de son expérience – **C:** rassurer – **D:** conseiller

www.quora.com

I am 16 years old and I feel really anxious about my future career because I do not know what to choose. What can I do?

Rick Patter Answered November, 10, 2020

.... There's no need to be anxious because you are too young to be sure of your decision.

.... When I was 16, I knew what I wanted to do, however when I got older, I realised that it was not the job for me. That's why I tried two other jobs before finding the perfect career.

.... So, relax and just look around. Try everything that interests you.

.... Trying again and again is the best way to find your dream career.

À vous de jouer!

Rédigez une réponse à cette même question en suivant les stratégies.

....

....

....

....

....

....

....

À retenir

A Connecteurs

Pour structurer votre écrit	Pour exprimer:	Pour ajouter une idée
– first/at first *d'abord* – then/next *ensuite* – finally *enfin* – to sum up *pour résumer* **Pour donner un exemple** – for example *par exemple* – like *comme*	**• la cause** – because *parce que* – because of *à cause de* – thanks to *grâce à* **• la conséquence** – so *donc* – that's why *c'est pourquoi*	– and *et* – moreover/in addition *de plus* **Pour opposer des idées** – but *mais* – however *cependant*

UNIT 6 Looking at the Past

PROJECT A2+

Your high school asks you to participate in a project to talk about past events that marked the world. Choose a period or an event and create a slide show to present it.

1 **Look at the picture and describe who and what you see. Guess the place and the period.**

2 64 **Listen and tick the right answer.**

a. The 8th edition of the Women's World Cup took place in: ☐ 2009 ☐ 2018 ☐ 2019

b. It was contested by: ☐ 12 teams ☐ 14 teams ☐ 24 teams

c. It started on: ☐ 7 June ☐ 17 June ☐ 7 July

d. It took place in: ☐ France ☐ the USA ☐ the Netherlands

e. The winner was: ☐ France ☐ the USA ☐ the Netherlands

f. They had already won the World Cup in: ☐ 1995 ☐ 2005 ☐ 2015

FLIPPED CLASSROOM

Find the words for the following definitions.

a. A fire that is burning strongly and out of control: ....

b. A sudden violent movement of the earth's surface: ....

c. A natural event such as wildfire or tsunami: ....

d. Go away from something or somewhere: ....

e. The opposite of leave: ....

1'30"
CAPSULE
Looking at the Past
foucherconnect.fr/21ptt37

UNIT 6

Periods Full of Surprises

ACTIVITY A Guess the News

LET'S GO FURTHER !!! →p. 68

1 65 **Fill in the news with the verbs below. Listen and check.**

devastated • won • became • announced • revealed

a. In February 2019, Lady Gaga .... an Oscar for Best Original Song.

b. On 10th April 2019, scientists .... the first image of a black hole in space.

c. On 15th April 2019, a large fire .... the Notre-Dame Cathedral in Paris.

d. In May 2019, Taiwan .... the first country in Asia to legalise same-sex marriage.

e. On 10th June 2019, French basketball player Tony Parker .... his retirement*.

*sa retraite

GRAMMAR SPOT

a. **They got married on 19th May 2018.**

b. **In February 2019, Lady Gaga won an Oscar.**

On utilise :

→ ☐ *in* ☐ *on: quand le jour est indiqué.*

→ ☐ *in* ☐ *on: quand il n'y a que le mois et/ou l'année.*

Training ex. 5 & 6 p. 70

2 **Match the news with the pictures.**

......

......

......

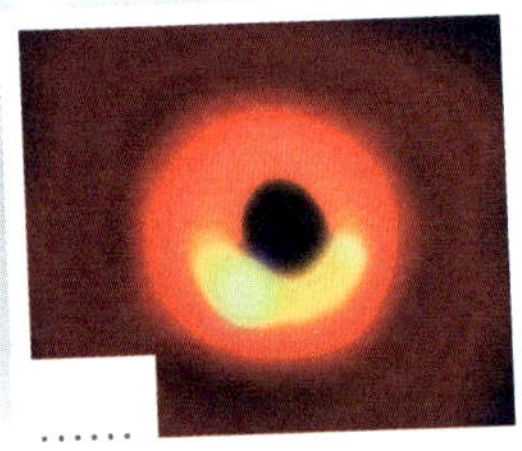
......

......

ACTIVITY B Royal Love Story

1 66 **Listen and complete the sentences with dates.**

a. In the ...., Meghan Markle and Prince Harry (*meet / met*) on a blind date[1] organised in London.

b. In ...., Harry (*propose / proposed*[2]) to Meghan.

c. They finally (*got married / get married*) on ...., and (*become / became*) the Duke and Duchess of Sussex.

d. On ...., Meghan (*gave / give*) birth to their first baby, Archie.

e. But the couple (*was / is*) not happy with living under the pressure of the media, especially paparazzi. So, in ...., the couple (*announced / announce*) they (*were / are*) planning to renounce their royal duties[3] in the United Kingdom, to live in North America.

f. In ...., the couple (*sign / signed*) a deal with Netflix to make films and TV shows.

WORD BOX

- **become*** devenir
- **happen** se dérouler, avoir lieu
- **meet*** rencontrer

1. *rendez-vous arrangé* ; 2. *demander en mariage* ; 3. *fonctions*

2 66 **Listen again and circle the verbs you hear.**

ACTIVITY C

Brexit Timeline

Brexit Key Dates

1. More and more British people wanted to leave the European Union so Prime Minister David Cameron promised to organise a referendum[1] on leaving the European Union (EU) or remaining in it.

2. British people voted for "Brexit" (**Br**itish **Exit**), to leave the EU.

3. Cameron resigned and Theresa May became the new Prime Minister.

4. After many negotiations between the EU and the British government, Theresa May didn't manage[2] to find an agreement and resigned, like Cameron. Boris Johnson became the new Prime Minister.

5. Johnson passed his agreement to organise Brexit and the United Kingdom officially left the EU.

2013 | .... | .... | .... | ....

1. Vote qui permet aux citoyens d'approuver ou de rejeter une proposition; 2. n'a pas réussi

1 (67) **Listen and fill in the missing dates in the timeline.**

2 Find in the timeline the English for:

a. *quitter* (§1): ....

b. *rester* (§1): ....

c. *a démissionné* (§3): ....

d. *un accord* (§4): ....

e. *a fait passer, a adopté* (§5): ....

GRAMMAR SPOT

a. **British people voted.**

b. **Theresa May became Prime Minister.**

Les verbes soulignés sont:
☐ *au présent* ☐ *au prétérit*

Le prétérit exprime une action:
☐ *en train de se dérouler*
☐ *passée, datée, terminée*

Training ex. 7 & 8 p. 70

3 Read the timeline and tick the right answer.

a. Where did Brexit happen? ☐ In the United Kingdom ☐ In Ireland ☐ In the USA

b. Which Prime Minister organised the referendum on Brexit? ☐ David Cameron ☐ Theresa May ☐ Boris Johnson

c. How many Prime Ministers resigned between 2013 and 2020? ☐ 1 ☐ 2 ☐ 3

d. When did the United Kingdom leave the European Union? ☐ In 2013 ☐ On 24 June 2016 ☐ On 31 January 2020

ACTION 1

Donner des informations sur des événements passés

A2 **Use the information below to record a presentation of cinema's key moments.**

- **May 1929: first Oscars ceremony.**
- **March 27, 1973: Marlon Brando, refusal of the Oscar for Best Actor.**
- **2010: Kathryn Bigelow, first female director to win an Oscar.**
- **2014: Ellen DeGeneres, historic selfie on Twitter with famous actors.**

UNIT 6

Years of Environmental Issues

ACTIVITY D Natural Disasters

1 Match these natural disasters with their French translation.

a. a wildfire • • 1. *la foudre (éclairs)*
b. a flood • • 2. *un feu de forêt*
c. a hurricane • • 3. *une inondation*
d. lightning • • 4. *un ouragan*
e. an earthquake • • 5. *un tremblement de terre*

2 Look at the cartoon and circle what you see.

the sun – the moon – stars – a wildfire – a flood – an earthquake – snow – rain – lightning – an eclipse – a hurricane/a tornado

3 Look again at the cartoon and tick True or False.

a. It's raining in summer. ☐ True ☐ False
b. There are wildfires in winter. ☐ True ☐ False
c. There are tornadoes in spring. ☐ True ☐ False
d. There is no difference between the four seasons. ☐ True ☐ False
e. The couple looks surprised. ☐ True ☐ False

WORD BOX

- **heavy** lourd, important
- **an issue** un problème
- **a storm** une tempête

4 Recap orally what you understood about the cartoon.

ACTIVITY E A Much Affected State

1 Look at the photos and describe what you see.

2 68 **Listen and complete the table with the missing information.**

Country: ....

State: ....

Number of disasters declared : ....

	❶	❷	❸
Date	....	From .... to	....
Disasters	....	Storm /	....
Damages	.... buildings destroyed and .... people killed	.... of acres* flooded	153,336 acres burned and .... people died

* *environ 1 demi-hectare*

ACTIVITY F Terrible Consequences

When Natural Disaster Strikes[1], Wildlife Pays a Heavy Price

The Amazon rainforest and Australia have made headlines[2] since September 2019; massive, uncontrollable fires in these regions have incinerated not only more than 26.4 million acres of land, but also more than a billion non-human animals[3]. University of New South Wales ecologist Chris Dickman conservatively estimates that 1.25 billion animals have died in the raging fires. [...]

Natural disasters impact non-human animals in many ways, not only by injuring and killing them. Disasters alter animals' physical environments and affect the many other plant and animal species on which they rely. Fires threaten animals with uncontrollable flames and heavy smoke; floods drown animals and contaminate water and food sources; hurricanes' and tornadoes' violent winds fling[4] heavy debris around and introduce diseases and toxins to new areas.

Lola Olvera, https://sentientmedia.org, March 25, 2020.

1. *frapper*; 2. *ont fait les gros titres*; 3. *animaux autres qu'humains*; 4. *jeter, lancer*

1 **Look at the picture and describe what you see. Guess the situation.**

2 **Read the text and tick the right answers.**

a. The document is about: ☐ earthquakes ☐ wildfires ☐ floods ☐ lightning
b. It deals with their impact on: ☐ the environment ☐ the economy ☐ technology

3 **Find the English for:**

a. *la faune et la flore* (title): ....
b. *lourd, important* (title): ....
c. *en blessant* (§2): ....
d. *menacer* (§2): ....
e. *noyer* (§2): ....
f. *des maladies* (§2): ....

4 **Tick True or False. Underline in the text to justify when it's false.**

a. 26.4 million acres of land were destroyed because of floods. ☐ True ☐ False
b. 1.25 billion animals died because of wildfires. ☐ True ☐ False
c. Natural disasters injure and kill animals. ☐ True ☐ False
d. Natural disasters don't impact on plants. ☐ True ☐ False

5 **Fill in the table with the consequences of each natural disaster.**

drown animals • introduce diseases • contaminate water • produce heavy smoke • fling heavy debris

Wildfires	....
Floods	....
Hurricanes and tornadoes	....

ACTION 2

STEP BY STEP → p. 60

MÉDIATION B1

Rassembler des informations de sources différentes et les résumer pour quelqu'un d'autre

Use the information from activities D, E and F to recap to your classmates how natural disasters have impacted the world over the years.

Differentiated Activities

LET'S GO FURTHER!!!

ACTIVITY A

p. 64

1 69 Listen to the document and write the name of the missing sports events under each picture.

a. ....

....

b. ....

....

c. ....

....

d. ....

....

e. ....

....

f. ....

....

2 69 Listen again and answer the questions.

a. What type of medal did Simone Biles win in 2019? ....

b. When did the Super Bowl happen? ....

c. How old was Ergan Bernal when he won the competition? ....

d. Who did Novak Djokovic beat? ....

e. Who is Stéphanie Frappart? ....

f. How many times did Lewis Hamilton win the US Grand Prix? ....

STEP BY STEP

ACTION 2

p. 67

Complete the sentences to recap how natural disasters have impacted the world over the years.

a. The first document (Activity D) is a cartoon that represents ....

....

b. The second document (Activity E) is an audio that explains what happened in ....

....

c. The last document (Activity F) is an article about ....

....

d. We can conclude that ....

....

TRAINING

AUDIO foucherconnect.fr/21ptt38

EXERCICES INTERACTIFS foucherconnect.fr/21ptt39

in TUNE

A 70 **Écoutez les nombres ci-dessous et répétez.**

1st – 2nd – 3rd – 4th – 5th – 20th – 31st

B 71 **Écoutez et entourez les nombres que vous entendez.**

a. 1 – 11 – 11th – 100 – 1st
b. 3 – 3rd – 30th – 3,000 – 30
c. 16 – 60th – 6 – 6th – 60
d. 21st – 32nd – 43rd – 55 – 55th

1 **Écrivez le nom de la catastrophe naturelle sous chacune des images.**

a. ....

b. ....

c. ....

d. ....

e. ....

2 **Entourez l'intrus et justifiez à l'oral.**

a. summer / winter / wildfire / spring
b. Theresa May / Lady Gaga / David Cameron / Boris Johnson
c. an earthquake / a hurricane / a flood / an agreement
d. April / Oscar / August / June

3 **Remplissez les mots croisés en traduisant les verbes demandés.**

Across →
2. *démissionner*
3. *donner naissance*
7. *se marier*
8. *rester*
9. *annoncer*

Down ↓
1. *quitter*
4. *avoir lieu*
5. *devenir*
6. *se passer*

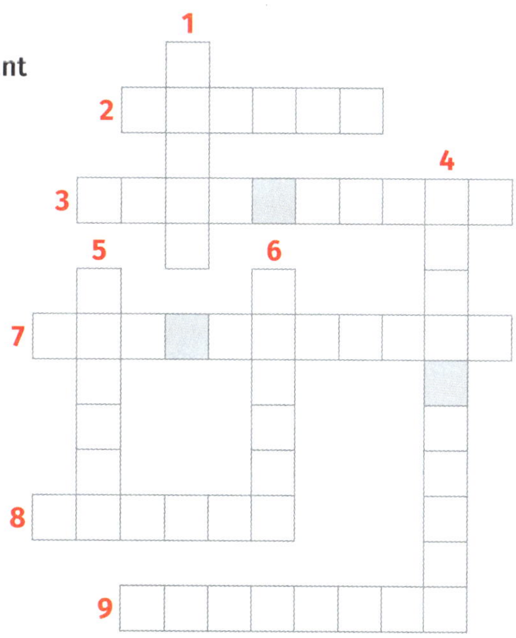

4 **Challenge!**

Vous avez 2 minutes pour faire autant de phrases possibles à propos des événements vus en classe.

5 Complétez avec la préposition qui convient.

a. Donald Trump became the 45th American President ..... January 2017.

b. The French astronaut Thomas Pesquet returned to Earth ..... 2017.

c. A lunar eclipse took place ...... July 27th 2018.

d. ...... July 7th 2019, the United States won the Women's World Cup.

e. Wildfires ravaged the Amazon rainforest ..... 2019.

6 72 Écoutez et complétez les dates manquantes.

a. On ...., Rafael Nadal won the French Open for the twelfth time.

b. The first Fortnite World Cup took place in ....

c. *Star Wars: The Rise of Skywalker* was premiered on ....

d. Famous basketball player Kobe Bryant died on ....

e. In ...., the "Disney +" streaming service was launched in France.

7 Conjuguez les verbes au prétérit.

a. France.............. the World Cup in 2018. (win)

b. French players .... four goals. (score)

c. The French coach .... the third man to win as a player and coach. (become)

d. Billions of people .... the game on TV. (watch)

e. The World Cup .... in Russia. (take place)

f. The tournament .... on June 14th 2018. (start)

8 Complétez en conjuguant les verbes suivants au prétérit.

launch • found • declare • create • become • want

a. At age 12, Elon Musk .... his first video game, called *Blastar*.

b. Later, he .... many companies, such as Space X and Tesla.

c. On March 24th 2006, Space X .... its first rocket: Falcon 1.

d. In 2011, Elon Musk .... he.................... to send humans to Mars.

e. In 2012, he .... a billionaire.

TIPS

LANGUAGE

Écrire et dire une date

En anglais britannique : jour avant mois

- **à l'écrit :** on 15(th) April 2019 *le 15 avril 2019*
- **à l'oral :** on the fifteenth of April, two thousand and nineteen

En anglais américain : mois avant jour

- **à l'écrit :** April 15(th) 2019 *le 15 avril 2019*
- **à l'oral :** on April (the) fifteenth, two thousand nineteen

Les prépositions

On 24 June 2016 *Le 24 juin 2016*
In June *En juin*
In 2016 *En 2016*
From 2018 to 2019 *De 2018 à 2019*

Le prétérit à la forme affirmative

On emploie le prétérit pour une action passée, datée et terminée.

Les verbes réguliers :
base verbale + -*ed*
A large fire devastated the Notre-Dame Cathedral.
Un grand feu a dévasté la Cathédrale de Notre Dame.

Les verbes irréguliers :
cf. rabat/liste
Lady Gaga won an Oscar.
Lady Gaga a gagné un Oscar.

UNIT 6

PROJECT

A2+

Present a Slide Show about Past Events

SCENARIO

Votre lycée vous demande de participer à un projet qui consistera à raconter des événements passés. Choisissez une période riche en événements ou un événement qui s'est déroulé sur plusieurs années et présentez-les à l'aide d'un diaporama.

A2

Rechercher des informations factuelles et pertinentes

- Choisissez au moins trois événements (faits divers, événements sportif, climatique, culturel, politique, cinématographique...) qui vous intéressent.
- Cherchez les informations concernant ces événements pour compléter la fiche ci-dessous.

→ Title of the chosen period: ....

→ Event n° 1
Name: ....
Date: ....
Place: ....
People: ....
What happened: ....

→ Event n° 2
Name: ....
Date: ....
Place: ....
People: ....
What happened: ....

→ Event n° 3
Name: ....
Date: ....
Place: ....
People: ....
What happened: ....

A2

Réaliser un diaporama

- Sélectionnez des illustrations correspondant aux événements choisis.
- Insérez-les dans chaque diapositive.
- Notez les mots-clés utiles à votre présentation sous chaque illustration.

A2+

Présenter des événements à l'aide d'un diaporama

- Préparez ce que vous allez dire pour chaque diapositive.
- Utilisez un dictionnaire en ligne pour vérifier la prononciation des mots nouveaux.
- Entraînez-vous à faire votre présentation orale en prenant appui sur les images du diaporama.

Auto évaluation

PORTFOLIO

foucherconnect.fr/21ptt40

UNIT 6

Accompagnement Personnalisé — Présenter un projet

Stratégies

1 Choisissez votre projet. Parmi les travaux réalisés tout au long de l'année ou de votre scolarité, sélectionnez un travail ou un projet ayant fait appel à l'utilisation de l'anglais.

2 Trouvez les informations pertinentes. Sélectionnez dans vos cours les documents et informations qui seront utiles pour préparer votre présentation orale. Lors de l'épreuve de l'examen, vous pourrez vous appuyer sur un support visuel.

3 Organisez vos idées. Listez vos idées sous forme de mots-clés ou plan d'intervention. Puis, faites un plan (introduction, développement et conclusion) pour les ordonner. Utilisez les éléments lexicaux étudiés ainsi que des mots outils A, B, C, D. Ne rédigez pas de phrases.

4 Entraînez-vous. Notez la prononciation des mots difficiles, puis répétez-les à l'aide de sites internet comme Wordreference. Enfin, chronométrez-vous afin que votre prise de parole corresponde aux 5 minutes requises.

Observation

73 **Écoutez le projet de Warren et complétez le plan ci-dessous avec les informations manquantes.**

- Subject: ......
- 1st idea: ......
- 2nd idea: ......
- 3rd idea: ......
- Conclusion: ......

À vous de jouer !

À partir des points de stratégie et de votre observation de la présentation de Warren, présentez le projet final ci-dessous.

- **Subject:** Celebration of the end of World War I in France and in the United Kingdom
- **1st idea:** Remembrance Day and the symbol of poppies[1]
- **2nd idea:** Armistice Day and the symbol of cornflowers[2]
- **3rd idea:** How we commemorated this day in our school
- **Conclusion:** the importance of remembering war victims

1. *coquelicots*; 2. *bleuets*

À retenir

A Pour présenter le sujet

- I've chosen to talk about... *J'ai décidé de parler de...*
- I would like to present... *Je souhaiterais présenter...*
- My presentation is about... *Ma présentation traite de...*

B Pour commencer une idée

- First... *Premièrement...*
- First of all... *Tout d'abord...*
- To start with... *Pour commencer...*

C Pour ajouter une idée

- Then... *Ensuite...*
- Therefore... *Donc, par conséquent...*
- Also... *Aussi...*

D Pour conclure

- To conclude/As a conclusion/In conclusion... *Pour conclure...*

CULTURE CLICK 3 HER MAJESTY QUEEN ELIZABETH II

a. ....

The Queen represents British people. She is Head of State of the UK, the Commonwealth[1] and the Church of England. But political .... are taken by Parliament and the elected ....

b. ....

She is the only British monarch to have reigned for more than 69 years. She began her reign on ....

c. ....

The Queen lives in Buckingham Palace, located in central .... The palace is made up of .... rooms.

d. ....

Her father was King George VI. The Queen married Prince Philip in .... They have four children: Charles, Anne, Andrew and Edward. They have .... grandchildren and .... great-grandchildren.

e. ....

She is the most popular and the most .... royal. She is often described as admirable, hard-working, ... and dedicated[2]. The celebration of her .... has always attracted vast crowds[3].

f. ....

She loves horse riding and .... (she is an Arsenal supporter!). She always has her .... by her side.

1. *le Commonwealth (organisation intergouvernementale composée de 54 états membres)*; 2. *dévouée*; 3. *de grandes foules*

1 **Look at the document and add the titles below.**

Her family • Her role • Her passions • Her reign • Her popularity • Her place of living

2 74 **Listen and fill in the missing information in the document above.**

3 75 **Match the dates and the royal events. Then listen and check.**

Dates

- a. 21 April 1926 •
- b. 1936 •
- c. 1945 •
- d. 2 June 1953 •
- e. 6 February 2017 •

Royal Events

- • 1. Abdication of Edward VIII (Elisabeth's uncle) and coronation* of George VI (her father)
- • 2. Princess Elizabeth's enrolment in the armed services as a driver and mechanic
- • 3. Birth of Princess Elizabeth
- • 4. Celebration of her Sapphire Jubilee (65 years of reign)
- • 5. Coronation* of the Queen

* *couronnement*

QUIZ

1. Queen Elizabeth's last name is:
- ☐ a. Cambridge
- ☐ b. Buckingham
- ☐ c. Windsor

2. The Queen's husband was:
- ☐ a. the King of England
- ☐ b. the Duke of Edinburgh
- ☐ c. the Prince of Wales

3. Queen Victoria (her great-great-grandmother) reigned from 1837 to:
- ☐ a. 1887 ☐ b. 1897 ☐ c. 1901

4. The motto* of the British monarchy is:
- ☐ a. Dieu et mon droit
- ☐ b. God Save the Queen
- ☐ c. England For Ever

5. Elizabeth II's coronation was fully televised and it was watched worldwide by an estimated:
- ☐ a. 77 million people
- ☐ b. 177 million people
- ☐ c. 277 million people

6. Queen Elizabeth has been served by:
- ☐ a. 9 UK Prime Ministers
- ☐ b. 14 UK Prime Ministers
- ☐ c. 19 UK Prime Ministers

7. She is the only person in the UK allowed to:
- ☐ a. ride a bike inside the palace
- ☐ b. ride her horse in every UK park
- ☐ c. drive without a licence

8. Her favourite dogs are:
- ☐ a. setters ☐ b. corgis
- ☐ c. Jack Russell terriers

9. For the London 2012 Olympic opening ceremony, she was seen in a film shot with Daniel Craig:
- ☐ a. parachuting from a helicopter
- ☐ b. taking part in a marathon
- ☐ c. playing polo

10. In the past 50 years, the Queen has worn about:
- ☐ a. 1,500 hats ☐ b. 5,000 hats
- ☐ c. 10,000 hats

** la devise*

76 Listen and check.

Your score: ..../10

3'24"
VIDÉO
Queen Elizabeth II Becomes Longest Reigning British Monarch in History
foucherconnect.fr/21ptt41

The Longest Reigning British Monarch in History

4 Watch the video from 0:14 to 0:34 and complete.

a. Queen Elizabeth II has surpassed her great-great-grandmother, Queen ...., to become the ....-serving British monarch in history.

b. The ....-year-old has reigned for .... years and 217 days. And it all began in the early ....s.

5 Watch the events that marked the year 1953 (from 0:34 to 1:12) and write True (T) or False (F).

a. The world discovered Ian Fleming's James Bond. (......)
b. Two mountaineers conquered Mount Everest. (......)
c. Elvis Presley started serving in the US Army. (......)
d. Five million people attended the coronation of the Queen in London. (......).

6 Watch from 1:12 to 1:49 and tick.

a. Elizabeth was: ☐ 25 ☐ 26 when she ascended to the throne.
b. Her father, George VI, became King after the: ☐ death ☐ abdication of his brother Edward VIII.
c. She became the first: ☐ monarch ☐ Head of State to circumnavigate* the globe.

** faire le tour du monde en bateau*

Will Prince William Succeed His Grandmother?

"When the queen dies, Prince Charles will automatically become king", Robert Hazell, a professor of government and the constitution at the University College London, told Insider. "So during William's lifetime, he will almost certainly see his father become king. Only if Charles dies before the queen, would William become king when the queen dies." [...] When William becomes king, Kate [Middleton] will become queen", Hazell said. [...] After Prince William, he and Middleton's eldest son Prince George is next in line for the royal throne. [...]. "[Their other children] Charlotte and Louis follow George in the line of succession."

Rachel Murphy, March 25, 2020, www.insider.com.

7 Read the article and explain in French what you have understood.

UNIT 7 Back from My Internship

PROJECT A2+

Returning from your internship, record a presentation of your work placement. Then share your information with one of your schoolmates and answer his or her questions.

1 **Observe the document and describe it orally.**

2 77 **Listen and complete the information about working in an open space office.**

a. Trainees can do their .... in different workplaces.

b. An .... office can offer many benefits during an internship.

c. This flexible structure helps trainees develop .... skills[1], knowledge[2] and creativity.

d. The trainee has very good working conditions to get ....

1. *des compétences*; 2. *des connaissances*

FLIPPED CLASSROOM

Watch the video and find the words corresponding to the definitions.

a. a person you work with: ....

b. a piece of work to be done: ....

c. all the people employed by a particular organization: ....

d. a temporary job to give work experience to a trainee: ....

1'30"
CAPSULE
Back from My Internship
foucherconnect.fr/21ptt42

UNIT 7

In the Workplace

ACTIVITY A — First Day on Work Placement

1 (78) **Listen to the conversation between Leo and Emma. Tick Right or Wrong.**

	Right	Wrong
a. Leo and Emma start work at 6.		
b. Leo is an intern at Barclays Bank.		
c. Emma works at Tesco, the big bakery in the High Street.		
d. Leo works in the administrative section.		

2 (79) **Listen to the end of their conversation. Cross out the incorrect information and correct it.**

a. On Monday, at Barclays there was a meeting at 8. ....

b. Leo wasn't active at all during the meeting. ....

c. At Tesco there were many tins to label. ....

d. Some salespeople weren't very understanding with Emma. ....

WORD BOX
- **label** étiqueter
- **a mentor** un tuteur
- **a tin** une boîte de conserve
- **understanding** compréhensif

ACTIVITY B — An Internship at Kew Gardens

1 (80) **Listen to Asher's internship interview. Fill in the question words. Then orally answer the questions.**

a. .... and .... were you on work placement?

b. .... was your work placement?

c. .... was your work schedule?

d. .... was your mentor?

2 (81) **Listen to the end of the interview. Select the information you hear.**

a. My mentor, Paul Smith, was very (*patient / friendly*).

b. He (*helped / coached*) me a lot with the plants.

c. The tasks were always (*varied / interesting*).

d. My favourite (*hobbies / tasks*) were creating new flower beds and growing (*trees / vegetables*).

GRAMMAR SPOT

a. **How was your first day? I wasn't passive. Some customers were very impatient. They weren't very understanding.**

➜ *Complétez la conjugaison de l'auxiliaire* **be** *au prétérit.*
– *I/he/she/it* ..../.................
– *You/we/they* ..../.................

➜ *Dans une question, l'auxiliaire se place :*
☐ *avant* ☐ *après le sujet*

b. **There was a meeting. There were many products to label.**

➜ *« Il y avait » se traduit soit par* «.....................» + nom singulier, *soit par* «.....................» + nom pluriel

Training ex. 4 & 5 page 82

ACTIVITY C A Summer Internship Experience

STEP BY STEP → p. 80

Hello, I'm Kevin Neal. This summer, I was an intern at the Center for Powerful Public Schools[1]. I had to get up early in the morning to get ready for work.

I was also able to become more accustomed to[2] dressing professionally more frequently. [...]
Arriving to work promptly[3] required me to figure out[4] when to leave my house to catch the bus on time. [...]
I was never given a task that I was incapable of accomplishing, but if there was ever something I needed clarification on then all I had to do was ask. [...]
I helped design a campaign for PREP 4 SUCCESS[5] and this is something that I am very glad I experienced.

Kevin Neal, http://powerfuled.org, August 17, 2017.

1. organisme de soutien aux écoles privées préparatoires à l'entrée à l'université; 2. s'habituer à; 3. rapidement; 4. m'a demandé de calculer; 5. programme de préparation à l'entrée à l'université

Read the document and tick the right answer.

a. Did Kevin get up early in the morning?
- ☐ Yes, he did. ☐ No, he didn't.

b. What type of clothes did he frequently wear?
- ☐ He always wore jeans. ☐ He often wore professional clothes.

c. How did he get to his internship?
- ☐ He didn't go to work on foot but he caught the bus.
- ☐ He caught the train.

d. What did he like best?
- ☐ He was very glad to design a campaign.
- ☐ He preferred attending a meeting.

GRAMMAR SPOT

a. **What __did__ he like best? __Did__ he __get__ up early in the morning?**
Yes, he __did__. No, he __didn't__.

b. **He __didn't__ __go__ on foot.**

Le temps employé est le:
☐ *prétérit* ☐ *présent* ☐ *futur*

À ce temps, comment se construit:
– une question?
(mot interrogatif) + ... + S + V + ... ?
– une phrase négative?
S + ... + V
– une réponse courte?
Yes, ... No, ...

Training ex. 6 & 7 page 82

ACTIVITY D A Day in the Life of a Bricklayer

1. The work was very physical. You need to be strong but I loved it.
2. Observing safety rules was essential, both for myself or for my co-workers.
3. We built a new house so I worked outdoors.

WORD BOX
- **attend** assister à
- **get* up** se lever
- **indoors** à l'intérieur
- **outdoors** à l'extérieur

82 **Listen and match the questions and the answers.**

a. Did you work indoors or outdoors? (......)

b. How did you like the job? (......)

c. What was the most important thing you learnt? (......)

ACTION 1

A2 **Poser des questions sur un stage et y répondre**

INTERNET www foucherconnect.fr/21ptt71

Work in pairs. In turn, play the role of the interviewer or the intern. Use the information on the cards to ask your partner information and to answer his/her questions about a previous internship.

ACTIVITY E A Convincing Work Experience

1'22"
VIDÉO
Lauren: A Day in the Life of a Vehicle Technician Apprentice
foucherconnect.fr/21ptt43

1 Watch the whole video and tick the right answer.

a. Lauren Cyster is a: ☐ vehicle technician ☐ mechanic
b. She started work at BT Fleet on the: ☐ 13th ☐ 30th of August.
c. Her co-workers are: ☐ professional ☐ brilliant
d. Lauren: ☐ doesn't like ☐ loves her job.

2 Watch the video from 0:18 to the end. Tick Right or Wrong.

	Right	Wrong
a. On her first day, she was told to take a blown engine apart* and put it all together again. That wasn't a very good learning experience.		
b. She helps on vans, trucks, cars and motorbikes.		
c. She recommends people go onto the website and have a look at the opportunities available.		
d. The job gave her the opportunity to show what she had learnt from all the other jobs she had done.		

* *démonter pièce par pièce un moteur grillé*

3 Orally recap what you have understood about Lauren's work placement.

ACTIVITY F Work Experience Impressions

LET'S GO FURTHER!!! → p. 80

a. ......
Oliver: During the first week of work, with the help of my supervisors I could adapt and feel more confident.

b. ....
Declan: I started a work placement in June as a part of my degree and I'm not really enjoying it.

c. ......
Ava: By observing and learning from my co-workers, I learned different types of skills.

d. ....
Emma: Getting this work placement seemed like it would be a great way to start my career but it isn't what I was expecting*.

e. ....
Owen: The problem lies in the fact that I really am not enjoying what I'm doing.

f. ......
Aria: Working on the project for the first week was enjoyable for me, as it made me use all the techniques I learned at school.

* *s'attendre à*

1 Read the statements above. Write a plus (+) when the statement is positive or a minus (-) when the statement is negative. Then underline part of the text to justify your opinion.

ACTIVITY G Enjoy Your Placement!

Struggling[1] on Your Placement Year? Don't Panic!

Remember that a work placement is a chance for you to see if the industry is the right workplace for you.

Use your placement as an opportunity to see if you enjoy a particular aspect of the industry you're hoping to enter, suggests Samantha Summers, 23, who graduated from the University of Gloucestershire last year.

"I didn't find coursework and assignments[2] that relevant, whereas my placement year gave me real hands-on experience – I'd never done marketing before and wasn't sure if I'd like it or not," she says.

If you're not enjoying your placement, then it doesn't have to be a waste of time. Maybe you've learned that you want a different career or workplace.

Louise Tickle, www.theguardian.com, 13 August 2014.

1. *être en difficulté, galérer;* 2. *les évaluations*

1 Observe the photo. Explain orally what you see and understand.

2 Read the article and tick the right answer.

a. The text is about: ☐ the importance of a work placement for a trainee ☐ the tutor who wants perfection

b. Samantha Summers is: ☐ giving a lecture ☐ giving advice to the students on work placement.

3 Find the English for:

a. *les devoirs scolaires* (§3): ....

b. *pertinent* (§3): ....

c. *une expérience de terrain* (§3): ....

d. *une perte de temps* (§4): ....

4 Underline in the text:

a. how a work placement in industry can help trainees form an opinion.

b. how trainees can use their work placements.

5 Read again paragraphs 3 and 4. Answer the questions.

a. What did Samantha Summers get from her placement year? ....

....

b. What can a bad experience reveal to a trainee? ....

....

....

ACTION 2

A2+ **Faire une description brève des bénéfices d'un stage**

List the benefits their work placements brought to Lauren, Oliver, Ava, Aria, Samantha.

Differentiated Activities

STEP BY STEP

ACTIVITY C

p. 77

1 Observe the speech bubble and write the information.

a. Intern's name: ....   b. Name of the company: ....

2 Read the text in the bubble and tick the right answer.

	Yes, he did.	No, he didn't.
a. Did he do his internship in winter?		
b. Did he work for an organization called The Center for Powerful Public Schools?		
c. Did he get up late in the morning?		

3 Read the text. Match the questions and the answers.

a. What type of clothes did he frequently wear? •
b. How did he get to his internship? •
c. Which task did he prefer? •
d. How did he like his internship? •

• 1. It was very useful for his future career.
• 2. Helping design a campaign.
• 3. He often wore professional clothes.
• 4. He didn't go on foot but he caught the bus.

LET'S GO FURTHER!!!

ACTIVITY F

p. 78

1 Imagine a justification to finish each sentence.

a. Oliver: I felt more confident because ....
b. Declan: I'm not really enjoying it because ....
c. Ava: I learned different types of skills because ....
d. Emma: It isn't what I was expecting because ....
e. Owen: I really am not enjoying what I'm doing because ....
f. Aria: It made me use all the techniques I learned at school because ....

2 Write a sentence to express your positive or negative opinion about your work placement and justify your answer.

....

....

AUDIO foucherconnect.fr/21ptt44

EXERCICES INTERACTIFS foucherconnect.fr/21ptt45

in TUNE

A 83 Écoutez et répétez.

were, weren't **/ɜː/** - where, wear **/eə/**

B 84 Entraînez-vous à prononcer les phrases suivantes. Écoutez et répétez.

a. Were you on work placement last month?
b. Where did you go on work placement?
c. What did you wear at work?
d. We weren't in the same office.
e. Where were you at lunchtime?
f. Yesterday, my supervisors weren't very friendly, they were very busy.

1 85 Complétez avec les mots correspondants. Écoutez et vérifiez.

a. an .... in an office

b. a .... / an ....

c. do a difficult ....

d. .... / colleagues

e. a .... / a tutor

2 Retrouvez dans la grille les équivalents anglais des mots de la liste ci-dessous.

Compétences
Connaissances
Formation
Horaires
Lieu de travail
Objectifs
Personnel
Rayon

W	K	T	N	F	Q	S	N	M	A
O	M	N	M	O	L	E	C	Z	S
R	B	L	O	A	I	R	F	C	L
K	P	J	O	W	R	T	H	J	L
P	D	G	B	Q	L	E	C	L	I
L	D	S	F	L	D	E	F	E	K
A	O	Q	M	U	O	L	D	N	S
C	J	H	L	H	D	J	D	G	D
E	K	E	S	T	A	F	F	G	E
O	S	G	N	I	N	I	A	R	T

3 Challenge!

Vous avez 2 minutes pour faire autant de phrases que possible avec les mots de la grille.

Training

4 Complétez les phrases avec *be* au prétérit, à la forme affirmative, négative ou interrogative.

a. Where .... you on work placement?
.... there many people in the company?

b. I .... in a small company and there .... many employees.

c. I .... in a big company and there .... many tasks to do. No time to get bored.

d. It .... a very good place of work for a first experience. I .... stressed at all.

5 86 Écoutez et complétez les phrases avec les mots que vous entendez.

a. .... did you work last year?
Personally, I .... in the same company as last year and the tasks .... easy at all.

b. I was in a small boutique and I loved .... I was. I didn't have to .... a uniform but I had to be smart.

c. At least my co-workers .... quite friendly and they helped me a lot.

6 Transformez les phrases suivantes à la forme négative pour expliquer ce que Steve n'a pas fait hier.

a. Yesterday, Steve greeted guests at his hotel. ....
....

b. He found taxis for the guests. ....
....

c. He helped the guests with their bookings. (*réservations*) ....
....

d. He made some calls. ....

7 À l'aide des illustrations, posez à Kevin des questions sur son stage. *Last month...*

a. ....
b. ....
c. ....
d. ....

TIPS LANGUAGE

Le prétérit

Exprime une action datée, passée, terminée.

Forme interrogative

Did + S + V + ...?

Did you like your last internship? *Est-ce que tu as aimé ton dernier stage ?*

Forme négative

S + didn't + V

Yesterday, I didn't take messages. *Hier, je n'ai pas pris de message.*

Forme affirmative *(voir unité 6)*

Be

I/He/She/It was / wasn't – Was he...?
We/You/They were / weren't – Were you...?

Were you in a big company last year? *Étais-tu dans une grosse entreprise l'an dernier ?*

No, I wasn't, I was in a small shop. *Non, j'étais dans un petit magasin.*

« Il y avait »

There was + nom singulier / *There were* + nom pluriel

There was a coffee machine. There were many co-workers. *Il y avait une machine à café. Il y avait beaucoup de collègues.*

UNIT 7

PROJECT A2+ Record a Presentation of Your Work Placement and Discuss It

SCENARIO

À votre retour de stage, vous enregistrez une présentation générale de votre stage en entreprise. Remettez cet enregistrement à l'un de vos camarades. Écoutez vos présentations respectives. Puis réalisez une courte conversation sous forme de questions-réponses.

A2 Compléter une fiche descriptive

- Complétez la fiche ci-dessous pour préparer les informations que vous présenterez.

→ My work placement from .... to ....

→ The company
Name: ....
Type: ....
Address: ....
Number of employees: ....

→ The staff
Mentor: ....
Colleagues: ....
Their attitudes: ....
....

→ Practical details
Working hours: ....
Transport: ....
Meals: ....
....

→ The workplace
Job: ....
Working hours: ....
Working conditions: ....
☐ outdoors ☐ indoors ☐ other

→ The tasks
Everyday tasks: ....
....
One special task: ....
....

→ Conclusion
What I liked / What I didn't like / What I learned:
....
....
....

A2+ Présenter un stage

- Utilisez les informations de votre fiche pour préparer la présentation orale de votre stage.
- N'écrivez pas de phrases mais entraînez-vous à répéter votre présentation.
- Enregistrez votre présentation.

A2+ Échanger des informations sur un stage

- Écoutez la présentation de l'un de vos camarades puis préparez quelques questions que vous lui poserez pour obtenir des informations complémentaires sur son stage.
- Posez vos questions à votre binôme et répondez aux siennes. Enregistrez votre conversation.

Auto évaluation
PORTFOLIO
foucherconnect.fr/21ptt46

UNIT 7

Accompagnement Personnalisé — Répondre à des questions

Stratégies

1 **Répondez de façon affirmative ou négative à une question fermée** qui commence par un auxiliaire en reprenant le sujet et l'auxiliaire.

2 **Répondez à une question ouverte** (introduite par un mot interrogatif) en vous appuyant sur la **signification du mot interrogatif** (nom, lieu, temps, etc.). A

3 **Développez votre réponse** en reformulant ce que vous avez compris, en donnant des exemples, des détails, en exprimant ou en justifiant votre point de vue. B

Observation

1 **Soulignez dans les réponses les éléments qui correspondent aux questions posées.**

a. Where did you do your internship?
I worked at Marks & Spencer from February to March.

b. What time did you start work?
Most of the time, I started work at 9.

c. Why did you choose this company?
I chose it because I wanted to learn how to repair cars.

d. When you were on work placement, how many tasks did you do?
I can't tell you how many tasks I did.
I did many different tasks.

e. Did you attend meetings? Yes, I did.

2 **Écrivez dans les parenthèses si les réponses aux questions ci-dessous expriment une cause, une opposition, un avis ou des exemples. Puis soulignez les éléments qui justifient votre réponse.**

a. Who is the man behind the front desk? I'm not sure. I think he is the new intern. → (..................)

b. When do your co-workers finish work?
My co-workers finish work at five but I work until 6. → (..................)

c. Where will you go on work placement next time?
I will go in a small shop because last time I was in a big supermarket. → (..................)

d. What did you do on internship? I greeted customers, I answered the phone, I made photocopies... → (..................)

À vous de jouer !

Utilisez les éléments proposés pour développer oralement des réponses aux questions suivantes. Puis continuez vos explications en ajoutant au moins un autre détail.

a. What time did you take the train to work? 7.30 am / start at 8.30 / 15 min. on foot

b. Where did you eat yesterday? at the cafeteria / good / cheap / no time / better than a sandwich

c. How many days is the new trainee staying? Three weeks / really wants to do well / more responsibilities during this week

À retenir

A Mots interrogatifs	B Indicateurs d'opinion
– What *quoi, que, qu', quel* – What time *(à) quelle heure* – Who *qui* – Where *où* – When *quand* – Why *pourquoi* – How *comment* – How much *combien (prix)* – How much + sing. / How many + pluriel *combien (quantité)* – How long *combien de temps* – How often *à quelle fréquence*	**Donner son avis :** – I think (that) *je pense que* – I agree / disagree with *je suis d'accord / pas d'accord avec* **Exprimer un contraste :** – but *mais* **Justifier :** – because, as *parce que, puisque*

UNIT 8 Customer Satisfaction

PROJECT A2+

You are dissatisfied with an item bought online on a British website. You call the company to complain.

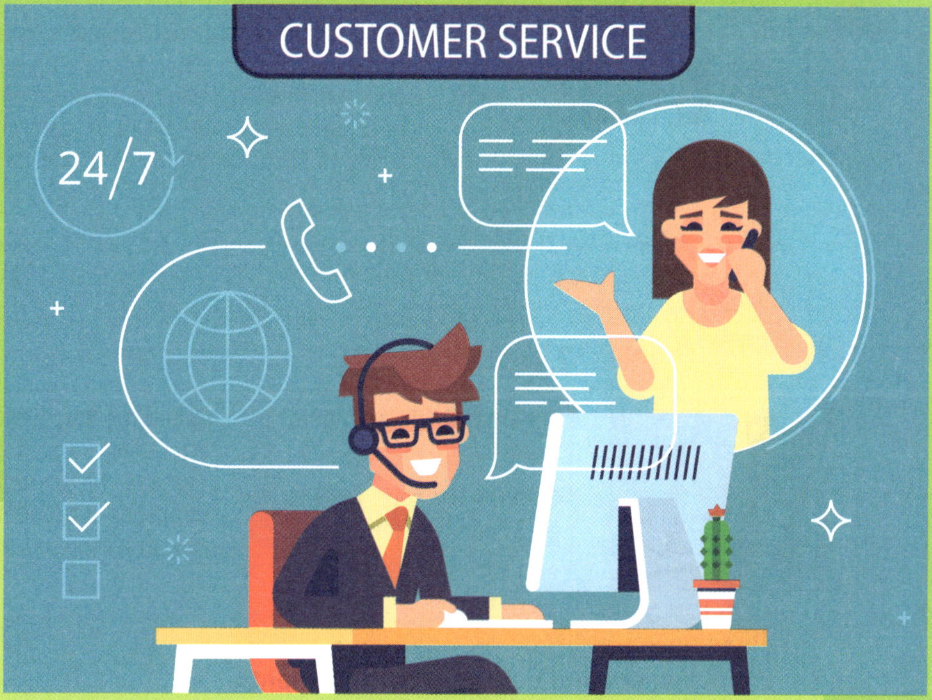

1 **Observe the document and describe orally what you see.**

2 **Classify the elements in the corresponding category.**

A – Reasons why a customer can be satisfied

B – Reasons why a customer can be dissatisfied

large choice of products (.....) • poor communication (.....) • poor customer service (.....) • fast service (.....) • rude[1] staff (.....) • bad quality of products (.....) • personalized service (.....) • occasional gifts[2] (.....)

1. grossier; 2. cadeaux

FLIPPED CLASSROOM

Watch the video and complete the definition.

.... is the assistance a company offers its .... after they use or buy its .... or services. It helps increase ....

1'30"
CAPSULE Customer Satisfaction
foucherconnect.fr/21ptt47

UNIT 8

Treat Yourself!

ACTIVITY A

Great Subscription Services

https://hellosubscription.com

1. Stitch Fix

Why we love it: Stitch Fix is like having your own personal stylist, except that you don't have to leave the house and you just have to wait for your new clothes and accessories to arrive in a box! They choose up to five clothing and accessory items just for you, based on the style profile you fill out upon signing up. It includes style, budget, and other specifics. [...] If there's something that doesn't fit you or something not in line with your fashion sense, you can return it without additional cost. Check out Stitch Fix Reviews to learn more about the service!

Price: The styling fee is $20 per month. If you decide to keep everything, you save 25% on your whole fix*.

* *sur l'ensemble*

www.mysubscriptionaddiction.com

2. Kinder Beauty

The Cost: $24.00 per month.
Subscribe here!

COUPON: Use code MSA5 to get $5 off your subscription!

About the Box: 100% vegan. Eco-friendly packaging. Curated with healthy beauty choices in mind. The Kinder Beauty Box is all about supplying subscribers with cruelty-free skincare, haircare, makeup, and other accessories!

1 **Look at the document and tick the correct elements.**

a. The documents are: ☐ advertisements ☐ letters
b. The two boxes offer: ☐ different products ☐ the same products
c. They: ☐ are ☐ are not the same price.

WORD BOX

- **eco-friendly** respectueux de l'environnement
- **a packaging** un emballage
- **subscribe** s'abonner

2 **Find the English equivalents for:**

a. *s'inscrire* (1): ....

b. *aller, être à la bonne taille (pour des vêtements)* (1): ....

c. *prix* (1): ....

d. *économiser* (1): ....

e. *abonnement* (2): ....

f. *fournir* (2): ....

3 **Read the first part of the document and tick True or False.**

a. When they choose the items, the stylists only pay attention to your fashion preferences. ☐ True ☐ False
b. You don't have to pay if you want to return some clothes. ☐ True ☐ False
c. You can decide to buy the clothes and accessories. ☐ True ☐ False

4 **Read the second part of the document and answer the questions.**

a. How much is the subscription if you use the coupon? ....

b. Why can we say that this box is environment-friendly? ....

....

ACTIVITY B Happy or Unhappy Customers?

1 87 **Listen and tick the correct elements.**

a. Andrea and Samuel are talking about their shopping: ☐ habits* ☐ budgets
b. They both prefer shopping: ☐ online ☐ in traditional shops

* *habitudes*

2 87 **Listen again and fill in the missing words.**

Advantages of online shopping	Possible drawbacks of online shopping
a. It is .... and easy to collect.	1. The .... has already been delayed twice.
b. The products are often a great	2. You can't .... the clothes on.
c. There is more	3. You can be disappointed with the .... or the fabric.
d. I love the great .... of brands.	

3 **Match the English words with their translation in French.**

a. a delivery •
b. an order •
c. to collect •
d. a brand •

• 1. *récupérer, passer prendre*
• 2. *une marque*
• 3. *une commande*
• 4. *une livraison*

GRAMMAR SPOT

a. I now prefer ordering online.
b. I enjoy receiving my orders.

Soulignez les verbes de sentiment. Que remarquez-vous sur le verbe qui suit ? ....
....

c. It is like having your own personal stylist.

« Like » se traduit ici par : ☐ *aimer* ☐ *comme*

d. They are not large enough.

Que remarquez-vous sur la place de enough ? ....
....

Training ex. 5 p. 92

ACTIVITY C Customer Satisfaction

1 **Watch the video and underline the correct elements.**

a. The video presents statistics about consumers' habits when they are (*satisfied / displeased*) with a purchase.
b. It explains that customer satisfaction has an impact on the (*brand / product*) image.
c. The consumers' communication about the products is (*more / less*) efficient than advertising campaigns and can lead to an increase in sales.

2 **Number the statistics in the order of the video, then fill in the percentages.**

☐ Share of satisfied consumers subscribing to email updates: ....%
☐ Share of consumers writing a positive letter or email about the brand: ....%
☐ Share of consumers following the brand on their social media channels: ....%
☐ Share of consumers writing online reviews: ....%
☐ Share of consumers joining loyalty programs: ....%

1'17"
VIDÉO
Why Is Customer Satisfaction Important?
foucherconnect.fr/21ptt48

ACTION 1

A2 **Présenter et donner son opinion sur une prestation de service**

Present your last online order and say if you were satisfied with it or not. Explain why.

Dealing with Commercial Problems

ACTIVITY D Commercial Documents

STEP BY STEP →p. 90

Philippi and Co
35 Anderson Road
BIRMINGHAM, BT1 1AR
Phone: 02895 8573780
Email address: philippi@ie.com

INVOICE

Customer address
Matt Shirley
343 Stratton Lane
SOLIHULL, SH33 6AA
Phone number: 0365 789 23 54
Email address: mshirley@bt.com ← ....

Invoice: 123 ← ....
Date: Feb 8, 2018 ← ....
Terms: Due upon receipt

DESCRIPTION	TOTAL
Flooring Removal Remove and dispose of existing wood floor	£900.00
Flooring Installation Install new hardwood floor. Price includes installation of a sub-floor and Brazilian Cherry hardwood	£6,000.00
5-year workmanship warranty	£0.00

← .... (Flooring Removal / Flooring Installation)

TOTAL	£6,900.00
Amount paid	£0.00
Amount due	£6,900.00

← .... (TOTAL / Amount due)

1 **Look at the document and say if this statement is true or false.**

An invoice gives information about what the customer has bought and how much he has to pay. ☐ True ☐ False

2 **Read the top and the bottom of the document and complete.**

a. Name of the company: ....

b. Name of the customer: ....

c. Amount of money already paid by the customer: ....

3 **Find the English equivalents in the document.**

a. *dû à reception* : ....

b. *enlèvement* : ....

c. *sous-plancher* : ....

d. *garantie* : ....

4 88 **Listen to the phone conversation between the company Philippi and Co and the customer. Correct the incorrect information on the invoice.**

GRAMMAR SPOT

a. **$750: seven hundred and fifty dollars**

b. **$6,750: six thousand seven hundred and fifty dollars**

➔ *Que remarquez-vous entre les centaines et les dizaines lorsqu'on lit ou écrit un nombre ?* ....
....

➔ *« Hundred » et « thousand » s'accordent-ils ici au pluriel ?* ....

Training ex. 1 & 2 p. 91

ACTION 2

Comprendre une conversation téléphonique à propos d'une commande A2

89 Listen to the phone conversation about the delivery of lunchtime menus and say in French what you understand.

ACTIVITY E A Dissastified Buyer

LET'S GO FURTHER!! →p. 90

www.reddit.com

Posted by u/vincent_vancough

Opinion **Buyer** **I bought a defective item and need an opinion on a fair refund.**

Discussion

I bought a receiver* on eBay. It was described as 'has been tested, works well'.
Well I received it and it turns on and plays music, but after about 10 seconds, it makes a loud pop and stops playing.
I documented this in a video and requested a refund from the seller. He responded and offered a refund for half of the cost.
I paid $50 + $25 shipping = $75 total.
He's offering a $25 discount, but I'm pretty sure that will not cover the repair cost. I want to ask for a full $50 refund so that I can get it repaired.
What do you think is fair? I don't want to be unreasonable.

14 comments Share Save Hide Report

3 years ago *Just return the item for a full refund including shipping. When the item is defective they have to pay for return shipping as well.*

VIEW ENTIRE DISCUSSION (14 COMMENTS)

* *un récepteur (pièce d'un Home Cinema)*

1 **Read the document and circle the name of the item bought. Then underline the problem with this item.**

2 **Find the English equivalents in the document.**

a. *un acheteur*: ....

b. *défectueux*: ....

c. *un vendeur*: ....

d. *un remboursement*: ....

e. *une remise/réduction*: ....

f. *des frais de port*: ....

3 **Answer the questions.**

a. How much was the item? ....

b. How much did the customer pay for the shipping? ....

c. What is the seller offering the dissatisfied buyer? ....

d. Does Vincent agree with this offer? ....

e. How many people commented on Vincent's post online? ....

4 **Draw a box around the proposition the seller made to Vincent.**

ACTION 3

A2

Rédiger un commentaire de consommateur

Add a comment to the discussion.

....

....

....

....

....

....

....

Differentiated Activities

STEP BY STEP

ACTIVITY D p. 88

1 90 **Listen to Part 1 and complete.**

– Hello, Philippi and Co, Suzie ....

– Hello, Matt Shirley speaking. I have a few questions about the .... I've just received.

– Sure, could you give me your invoice .... ?

– Yes, it's invoice n° ....

– All right, I've found it. Can I check your ...., please?

– Yes, of course, it's 343 Stratton Lane in Solihull.

– That's OK. And your ...., please?

– 0365 789 23 54

– OK. Thank you. Lastly, what is your .... address?

– m.shirley@bt.com

– Fine. So what are your questions?

2 91 **Listen to Part 2 and tick the correct elements.**

a. The first problem is the:
- ☐ amount
- ☐ date of the invoice

b. The second problem is the price of the flooring:
- ☐ removal
- ☐ installation

c. The price of the flooring removal is:
- ☐ 150
- ☐ 750 dollars

d. The disposal of the flooring was done by:
- ☐ Philippi and Co
- ☐ Matt

LET'S GO FURTHER!!!

ACTIVITY E p. 89

0'58"
VIDÉO
How to Return your Amazon Purchase for Free
foucherconnect.fr/21ptt49

1 **Watch the video and say what it is about.**

....

2 **Answer the questions.**

a. What is the first thing to do to return a purchase?

....

b. What is it necessary to print?

....

c. What are these two documents for?

....

....

d. When will you get your refund?

....

3 **Make a summary of the video in French.**

....

TRAINING

AUDIO foucherconnect.fr/21ptt50

EXERCICES INTERACTIFS foucherconnect.fr/21ptt51

in TUNE

A 92 **Écoutez et répétez:** like **/ai/ – hate /ei/**

B 93 **Classez ces mots en fonction de leur prononciation, puis écoutez et vérifiez.**

subscribe • price • mind • pay • item • information • online • buy • label • contain

/ai/	/ei/
....	....
....	....

1 **Écrivez les nombres en toutes lettres.**

a. 13 ....

b. 87 ....

c. 145 ....

d. 678 ....

e. 1,459 ....

2 **Complétez ces opérations.**

a. eleven + sixty-seven = ...

b. forty-eight × .... = ninety-six

c. .... – thirty-seven = a hundred

d. three hundred and thirty-three: three = ...

3 **Écrivez les mots correspondant à chaque image.**

a defective item • a mistake in the order • late delivery • a refund • too large • not large enough

a. ....

b. ....

c. ....

d. ....

e. ....

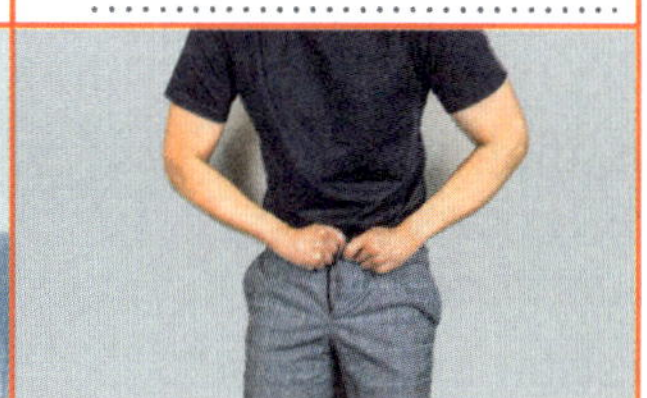

f. ....

4 **Challenge!**

Citez le plus de raisons possibles pour lesquelles un client peut être mécontent d'un achat.

5 **Soulignez la forme qui convient.**

a. Jen loves (*window-shop / window-shopping*) every Saturday afternoon.
b. Joshua can't stand (*try / trying*) clothes on in shops.
c. Could you (*give / giving*) me your email address?
d. They don't like (*spend / spending*) too much time on the Net.
e. The first thing to do is to (*log in / logging in*).

6 94 **Écoutez et complétez.**

– Hello, Home Company, Paula ....
– Hello, I'm calling to get .... about an order.
– Could you please give the order ....?
– Sure, it's .... 789.
– Thank you. Well, you placed an .... for a dishwasher.
– Yes, that's it but the problem is that it has not been .... yet.
– Really? The delivery date was ....
– Indeed, it was.
– Well, I'm going to contact the delivery .... to understand the reason for the .... and I'll be back in touch with you as soon as possible.
– OK, thank you.

7 **Traduisez en anglais.**

a. Si vous n'êtes pas satisfait de votre achat, demandez un remboursement.

....

....

b. Pour retourner un article, vous devez imprimer une étiquette retour.

....

....

c. Ce tee-shirt n'est pas assez grand.

....

....

d. Ce produit est trop cher.

....

....

LANGUAGE TIPS

Les verbes de sentiment

– Pour dire ce que l'on aime, on utilise les verbes *like*, *enjoy* ou *love*.

– Pour dire ce que l'on n'aime pas, on utilise *I don't like / I dislike* (je n'aime pas), *I hate* (je déteste), *I can't stand* (je ne supporte pas).

– Pour dire ce qui importe peu, on utilise *I don't mind* (ça m'est égal).

– Pour dire ce que l'on préfère entre différentes options, on utilise *I prefer*.

Ces formes verbales sont suivies d'un nom ou d'un verbe en *–ing*.

I can't stand customer reviews, they're always so negative. *Je ne supporte pas les avis de consommateurs, ils sont toujours si négatifs.*

I like going shopping with my sister on weekends. *J'aime faire les magasins avec ma sœur le weekend.*

Les nombres

67 → sixty-seven
On met un tiret entre les dizaines et les unités.

147 → one/a hundred and forty-seven
On emploie *and* devant les dizaines et les unités.

2,654 → two thousand six hundred and fifty-four
Les chiffres des milliers (millions, milliards) sont séparés par une virgule.

UNIT 8 PROJECT A2+

Make a Phone Complaint

SCENARIO

Vous êtes mécontent d'un article acheté sur un site britannique. Vous téléphonez pour vous plaindre.

A2

Compléter un bon de retour

- Complétez le bon pour détailler votre commande et expliquez le motif de votre mécontentement.

→ Item: ....

→ Price: ....

→ Order date: ....

→ Order reference: ....

→ Delivery date: ....

→ Shipping fees: ....

→ Reasons for your dissatisfaction: ....

....

....

....

....

→ You would like ☐ an exchange
☐ a refund
☐ other: ....
....

A2+

Effectuer une réclamation orale

- Préparez la conversation téléphonique avec un camarade de classe à partir du bon de retour.
- Distribuez les rôles : client mécontent / personnel du service après-vente.
- Préparez un story-board et indiquez en quelques mots l'objet de chaque réplique.
- Simulez la conversation téléphonique.

Auto évaluation

PORTFOLIO

foucherconnect.fr/21ptt52

Répondre à une plainte

Stratégies

1 Écoutez votre interlocuteur pour comprendre la plainte. A

2 Présentez vos excuses. B

3 Proposez une solution ou un arrangement, ou indiquez au client que sa plainte n'est pas justifiée et expliquez-lui pourquoi. C

4 Remerciez votre interlocuteur. D

À vous de jouer !

96 Vous êtes en PFMP dans une entreprise et vous recevez l'appel d'un client mécontent. Écoutez et réagissez en utilisant les éléments suivants.

- Ask the customer the reference of the order.
- Find out the problem.
- Tell her that the delivery has been delayed and that the package will arrive at her home at the end of the week.
- Apologise for the delay.
- Tell her that you will refund the shipping fees.
- Thank her and say goodbye.

Observation

95 **Écoutez ce message téléphonique et complétez avec :**

replace • discount • broken • complain • apologies.

"Good morning, Sir. We acknowledge receipt of your email dated 6th April in which you .... about the late delivery and .... items in order n° AD/564. First of all, please accept our sincere .... for the inconvenience caused. In order to compensate, we are prepared to .... the damaged goods free of charge and shall be pleased to grant you a 10% .... on your order. We hope that such an unfortunate incident will not compromise our future business relations. Could you please contact us to say if this suits you? Thank you, and have a nice day."

À retenir

A Demander la nature de la plainte

- What can I do for you? *Que puis-je faire pour vous ?*
- What's the problem? *Quel est le problème ?*
- What is wrong? *Qu'est-ce qui ne va pas ?*
- How can I help you? *Comment puis-je vous aider ?*
- What is your order reference? *Quelle est la référence de votre commande ?*

B Présenter des excuses

- Please accept our sincere apologies for the inconvenience you have been caused. *Veuillez accepter nos excuses les plus sincères pour le dérangement que vous avez subi.*
- We apologise once again for the inconvenience caused. *Nous renouvelons nos excuses pour les problèmes que vous avez eus.*
- We would like to apologise for the delay. *Nous aimerions nous excuser pour le retard.*
- We are sorry for the mistake. *Nous sommes désolés pour l'erreur.*

C Proposer une solution

- In order to compensate... *À titre de compensation...*
- We shall be pleased to grant you a discount. *Nous serons heureux de vous proposer une réduction.*
- We will give you a 5% discount. *Nous allons vous offrir une réduction de 5 %.*
- Would you like to exchange it? *Aimeriez-vous l'échanger ?*

D Remercier

- Thank you so much for... *Merci beaucoup de / pour...*
- I would like to thank you (very much indeed). *Je souhaite (vraiment) vous remercier.*
- See you again soon, I hope. *À bientôt, je l'espère.*

CULTURE CLICK 4 EVOLUTION OF MUSIC IN THE UNITED STATES

17th – 18th ....

Slaves brought their African native songs to America. These songs turned into negro spirituals and by the mid-1830s, gospel.

End of 1800s – beginning of 1900s

Blues appeared in the .... and the .... of the USA.

....

Jazz was invented. Billie Holiday, Nina Simone and Ella Fitzgerald are representatives of the genre.

1950s

This period marked the start of rock and roll. Elvis Presley recorded his first .... in 1953.

....

British bands the Rolling Stones and the Beatles conquered the American audience.

Mid-1980s

Rap emerged with strong ....

....

Michael Jackson sold 25 million copies of *Thriller*.

1990s

People saw the start of grunge with .... such as Nirvana.

Today

One of the icons of ...., ... and .... is Beyoncé.

1 97 **Listen and fill in the timeline about the evolution of music.**

2 97 **Listen again and match the artists with the musical genre.**

a. Billie Holiday, Nina Simone and Ella Fitzgerald •	• 1. Blues
b. Public Enemy •	• 2. Rock and Roll
c. Elvis Presley •	• 3. Rap
d. Johnny Lee Hooker •	• 4. Jazz

CULTURE CLICK 4 EVOLUTION OF MUSIC IN THE UNITED STATES

QUIZ

1. **The American music awards show is:**
   - ☐ a. the Brit Awards
   - ☐ b. the NRJ Music Awards
   - ☐ c. the Grammy Awards
2. **What does CMA stand for?**
   - ☐ a. the Cultural Music Association
   - ☐ b. the Country Music Association
   - ☐ c. the Cinema and Music Association
3. **The all-time best-selling band is:**
   - ☐ a. the Beatles
   - ☐ b. the Dave Matthews Band
   - ☐ c. Queen
4. **The first commercial CD was produced in:**
   ☐ a. 1982 ☐ b. 1986 ☐ c. 1989
5. **The youngest artist to have received a Grammy is:**
   - ☐ a. Billie Eilish
   - ☐ b. LeAnn Rimes
   - ☐ c. Britney Spears
6. **Jimmy Hendrix is known for playing:**
   - ☐ a. the bass
   - ☐ b. the guitar
   - ☐ c. the drums
7. **The Woodstock Festival took place in:**
   ☐ a. 1959 ☐ b. 1969 ☐ c. 1979
8. **The Grammy Award for Best Music Video was created in:**
   ☐ a. 1944 ☐ b. 1984 ☐ c. 1974
9. **On Spotify, the most listened-to song is:**
   - ☐ a. "Yesterday"
   - ☐ b. "Shape of You"
   - ☐ c. "Havana"
10. **"Oh Happy Day" belongs to the genre of:**
    - ☐ a. R&B
    - ☐ b. pop
    - ☐ c. gospel

98 **Listen and check.**

Your score: ..../10

3'53"
VIDÉO
How BTS and K-Pop disrupted mainstream politics
foucherconnect.fr/21ptt53

3 **Watch the video from 1:49 to 2:41 and tick the correct answer.**

a. K-pop roots are: ☐ cultural ☐ business

b. The K-pop industry emerged from financial crisis in the late: ☐ 1980s ☐ 1990s

c. To rebuild the economy, the government invested in: ☐ agriculture ☐ entertainment

d. Global sales for K-pop related music and video grew to earn $5 billion: ☐ a month ☐ a year

e. In 2015, South Korea started blaring K-pop music across the border towards: ☐ North Korea ☐ Japan

4 **Watch the video from 3:16 to the end and answer the questions.**

a. What band spoke to the United Nations?

....

b. How many members are in the band?

....

c. What campaign did they create?

....

NIRVANA

Kurt Cobain [was an] American rock musician who rose to fame as the lead singer, guitarist, and primary songwriter for the seminal grunge band Nirvana.

Cobain and Krist Novoselic formed Nirvana in 1987. [...] With new drummer Dave Grohl (who joined the band in 1990), Nirvana released[1] its major-label debut, *Nevermind* (1991), which featured the hit single "Smells like Teen Spirit"; it became the first alternative-rock album to achieve widespread[2] popularity with a mainstream audience. *Nevermind* catapulted Nirvana to worldwide fame [...].

Cobain's death marked, in many ways, the end of the brief grunge movement and was a signature event for many music fans of Generation X. He remained an icon of the era after his death and was the subject of a number of posthumous works.

www.britannica.com.

1. *a sorti*; 2. *très grand, étendu*

5 **Explain in French what you have understood about the document.**

UNIT 9 Social Networks and Teens

PROJECT B1

For National Media Day, your class is organising a survey to evaluate the uses of social media by their fellow pupils.

Instagram and Snapchat, American teenagers' favourite social media

% of American teenagers choosing the following social media as their favourite

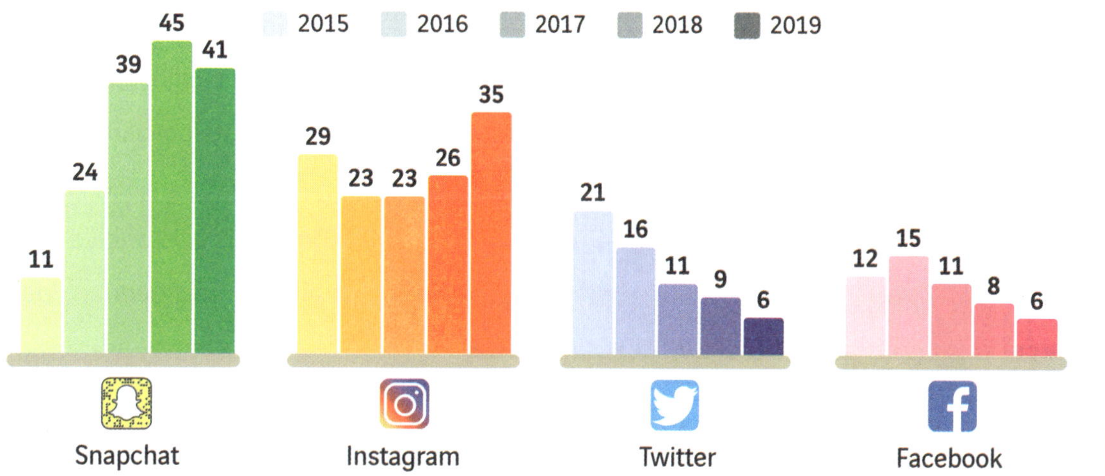

https://au.pcmag.com.

1 **Look at the diagram and explain it (subject, percentage, evolution, social networks...).**

2 99 **Listen and match each social network with its use.**

a. Snapchat •
b. Instagram •
c. Twitter •
d. Facebook •

• 1. People write very small messages to express their opinions.
• 2. People mostly post pictures.
• 3. People connect with friends and family and can post videos, photos and texts.
• 4. People can post videos or pictures which are made public for a short time.

FLIPPED CLASSROOM

Fill in with the correct word.

a. When you write a message on a social network and send it, you .... it.

b. You .... your phone when you spend time reading the posts on your app.

c. .... is bullying with the use of digital technologies.

d. The .... keeps you up to date* with what happens to people you follow on social media.

* *tenir au courant*

1'30"
CAPSULE
Social Networks and Teens
foucherconnect.fr/21ptt54

UNIT 9

The Use of Social Media

ACTIVITY A Addiction? Did You Say Addiction?

www.cdc.gov.

1 Tick the correct answers.

a. What is the poster about? ☐ time spent on screen by teenagers ☐ time spent doing outdoor[1] activities

b. What is the age group? ☐ 13-16 ☐ 15-18 ☐ 16-18

c. How long do teenagers spend in front of a screen?
☐ 6 hours a week ☐ 7½ hours a week
☐ 7½ hours a day

d. What do teenagers do for 4½ hours a day?
☐ play video games ☐ listen to music ☐ watch TV

e. What are the suggested activities to replace screen time? ☐ play football ☐ walk the dog
☐ go for a walk ☐ do yard[2] work

f. Who does this poster give advice to?
☐ pupils ☐ teachers ☐ parents

1. *extérieur*; 2. *jardin*

2 Answer these questions orally.

a. How much time a day do you spend scrolling through your telephone?
b. Do you consider yourself to be addicted?

GRAMMAR SPOT

a. **How often are you connected to social media?**
b. **How many times a day do you post new content?**
c. **The team always uses social media.**
d. **I post new content once or twice a day.**

→ *Entourez les mots interrogatifs dans les questions a et b. Ils se traduisent par :*
....
→ *Soulignez l'adverbe de fréquence dans la phrase c. Où est-il placé ?* ....
→ *Soulignez l'expression de la fréquence dans la phrase d.*

Training ex. 6, 7 & 8 p. 104

ACTIVITY B Professional Use

1 (100) Listen and number the questions in the correct order. Then underline the correct answers.

...... What does your job consist of? *Creating a community around a product, a brand or a charity / Selling products to customers.*

...... How many times a day do you post new content? *Once or twice / Two or three times.*

...... How often is your team connected to social media? *Sometimes / Always.*

2 (100) Listen again and orally explain what a community manager does and what you have understood.

ACTIVITY C Positive Aspects of Social Media

Charitable Giving Demographics For Nonprofits[1]

Millennials:[2]

- [are] 25.9% of US population.
- 40% of millennial donors are enrolled in a monthly giving programme.
- 26% give tribute gifts[3].
- 46% donate to crowdfunding campaigns. [...]
- 16% give through Facebook fundraising tools.
- 64% volunteer locally, 9% internationally.
- 55% attend fundraising events.
- 11% of total US giving comes from Millennials.
- 84% of Millennials give to charity, donating an annual average of $481 across 3.3 organizations.
- Millennials are active on their phones and respond best to text message and social media, but rarely check personal email or respond to voice calls.
- Millennials are most likely to contribute to work-sponsored initiatives, donate via mobile and watch online videos before making a gift.

https://nonprofitssource.com.

1. des données démographiques concernant les dons aux organismes à but non lucratif; 2. une personne devenue adulte aux alentours de l'an 2000; 3. des dons

1 Present the document orally (title, source and topic).

2 Find the English equivalents in the document.

a. *sont inscrits (à)*: ....

b. *des campagnes de financement participatif*:

....

c. *des outils pour collecter des fonds*:

....

d. *une moyenne*: ....

e. *ont plus tendance à*: ....

WORD BOX

- **an addiction** une dépendance
- **a brand** une marque
- **a charity** une association caritative
- **a consumer** un consommateur
- **screen time** temps passé sur écran

3 Underline the correct element.

a. Millennials (*are / aren't*) active on their phones.

b. They (*use / don't use*) text messages and social media.

c. They mostly (*respond / don't respond*) to voice calls.

d. Millennials (*contribute / don't contribute*) best to work-sponsored initiatives.

e. They (*give / don't give*) gifts via email.

ACTION 1

Poser et répondre à des questions sur l'utilisation des réseaux sociaux A2+

Using Activities A, B and C, ask your partner several questions about the different uses of social media and answer his/her questions.

Social Media: Friend or Enemy?

ACTIVITY D

Disconnecting from Social Media

VIDÉO 2'34"
The Social Dilemma – Official Trailer
foucherconnect.fr/21ptt55

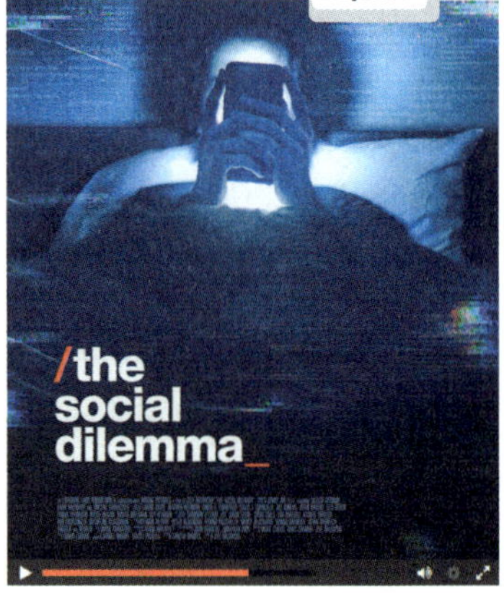

1 Watch the video and use the elements below to present it orally.

The document is a (...). The title is (....). It is broadcast on (...). The topic is (...).

2 Watch from the beginning to 0:46 and tick the right answers to sum up the main message.

The man interviewed wants people to know that: ☐ everything ☐ nothing they're doing on line is being: ☐ switched ☐ watched, is being: ☐ tracked ☐ packed.

Every single action that they take is being carefully: ☐ monitored ☐ mirrored ☐ recorded.

The people interviewed worked for : ☐ Twitter ☐ Facebook ☐ TikTok ☐ Pinterest ☐ Instagram ☐ Snapchat ☐ Google

3 Watch from 1:10 to the end and complete with the words below.

control • affect • emotions • fake news • completely • effective • Facebook • population

a. .... discovered they were able to .... real world behaviour and .... without ever triggering[1] the users' awareness[2].

b. They [the users] are .... clueless[3].

c. .... spreads[4] six times faster than true news.

d. We have less .... over who we are and what we really believe.

e. If you want to control the .... in your country there has never been a tool as .... as Facebook.

1. *déclencher*; 2. *prise de conscience*; 3. *n'ont pas la moindre idée*; 4. *se répandre*

4 Tick True or False and justify.

a. Every action is tracked on line. ☐ True ☐ False ....
....

b. Teenagers are more anxious and depressed because of social media. ☐ True ☐ False ....
....

c. Social media users are aware of being manipulated.
☐ True ☐ False ....

d. People are invaded by fake news. ☐ True ☐ False
....

e. Twitter is an effective tool to control populations.
☐ True ☐ False ....
....

5 Orally sum up what you have understood about the video.

GRAMMAR SPOT

a. Millennials are 25.9% of the US population.

b. 1/4 describe its effect as negative.

c. Roughly three in ten teens say social media has a positive impact.

➜ *Soulignez le pourcentage. Il se dit:*
....

➜ *1/4 se dit, en anglais britannique:*
☐ *a/one quarter*
☐ *one in fourth*

➜ *Entourez la donnée chiffrée dans la phrase c.*
Elle se traduit en français par:
....

Training ex. 4 & 5 p. 104

ACTIVITY E What Is Online Bullying? LET'S GO FURTHER!!!

→p. 102

How much do you know about cyberbullying?

1. **What is cyberbullying?**
   a. an email by a friend
   b. a smack in your face
   c. a threatening[1] message
2. **How often do you check your messages on social media?**
   a. once a day
   b. twice a day
   c. every 5 minutes
3. **What do you do when someone sends you a threatening email?**
   a. I start crying
   b. I face the problem alone
   c. I tell my parents
4. **How often do you check the profile of a friend request?**
   a. never
   b. 50% of the time
   c. always
5. **What is the best reaction to cope[2] with cyberbullying?**
   a. not doing anything about it
   b. protecting your accounts
   c. reaching out for help

1. menaçant; 2. faire face

Circle your answers, count the number of a, b and c you have and check your results.

INTERNET
foucherconnect.fr/21ptt56

ACTIVITY F A Survey About Social Media STEP BY STEP

→p. 102

1 101 **Listen and present the document (type of document, topic, age group, date of publication).**

....

2 101 **Listen again and fill in the blanks with the statistics.**

a. The results say that .... of teens have access to a smartphone, and .... say they are online almost constantly.

b. 45 % believe social media has no effect on people their age. Roughly .... teens say social media is positive while .... describe its effect as negative.

c. Amongst the negative effects, ... of these teens explain that social media has led to more bullying and rumours.

3 **Underline the mistakes and correct the sentences.**

a. A minority of teens have access to a smartphone. → ....

b. One in twenty teens say social media has a positive impact. → ....

c. 45% believe social media is negative.
→ ....

d. For more than fifty percent of teens, social media has led to more bullying and rumours. → ....

ACTION 2

B1 **Résumer des informations factuelles sur les dangers des réseaux sociaux**

Write a short paragraph using the information from activities D and F to recap what you have understood about some of the dangers of social media.

Differentiated Activities

LET'S GO FURTHER!!!

ACTIVITY E p. 101

VIDÉO 4'39''
The Cyber Bullying Virus
foucherconnect.fr/21ptt57

1 Watch the second video on the web page from the beginning to 0:30 and answer the questions.

a. What do human beings crave[1]? ....

b. What helps people satisfy their social appetites? ....

1. *désirer*

2 Watch from 0:30 to 1:32 and complete the sentences.

Cyber bullying is the use of online communication to harass, threaten or .... another. The action of cyber bullying can vary from forwarding cruel private ...., pictures or videos to assuming false .... on social networking sites. [...] Cyber bullies have the advantage of ...., masked behind their computer screen and .... accounts. Many are given a false sense of .... and security, believing that their actions will have no ....

3 Watch the video from 1:32 to 1:59 and answer the questions.

a. What symptoms can victims experience? ....

....

b. What creature is cyber bullying like? ....

c. Who can put an end to this problem? ....

4 Watch from 2:00 to the end and orally sum up what you have understood.

STEP BY STEP

ACTIVITY F p. 101

1 102 Listen and circle the correct answer.

a. The document is a (*TV show / radio show*).

b. The teens questioned in the survey were (*13-15 / 13-17*) years old.

2 102 Listen again and tick the correct answer.

a. The results say that: ☐ 85 % ☐ 95% of teens have access to a smartphone, and: ☐ 45% ☐ 55% say they are online almost constantly.

b. 45 % believe social media has no effect on people their age. Roughly: ☐ two in ten ☐ three in ten teens say social media is positive, while: ☐ 1/4 ☐ 3/4 describe its effect as negative.

c. Amongst the negative effects, ☐ 7% ☐ 27% of these teens explain that social media has led to more bullying and rumours.

3 Say if the sentences are true (T) or false (F).

a. A majority of teens can't access a smartphone. ......

b. 1/20 says social media has a positive impact. ......

c. 25% of teens think social media has negative effects. ......

d. For more than a quarter of teens, social media has led to more bullying and rumours. ......

TRAINING

AUDIO foucherconnect.fr/21ptt58

EXERCICES INTERACTIFS foucherconnect.fr/21ptt59

in TUNE

A 103 **Écoutez la prononciation de la lettre « c » dans les mots suivants.**

calls **/k/** social **/ʃ/** cyber **/s/**

B 104 **Classez les mots selon leur prononciation. Écoutez et vérifiez.**

consumer • decline • distancing • security • socialise • society • cinema

/k/	/ʃ/	/s/
....	....	....
....	....	....
....	....	....

1 **Retrouvez la traduction des mots suivants dans la grille.**

réseaux sociaux • association caritative • campagne • cyber-harcèlement • envoyer un SMS • fil d'actualité • temps d'écran

S	O	C	I	A	L	M	E	D	I	A	G	F	N
B	A	H	D	S	H	E	T	R	A	Q	D	P	E
D	S	A	G	Z	J	D	T	P	E	C	T	M	W
S	C	R	E	E	N	T	I	M	E	Z	Y	N	S
O	V	I	F	T	F	Z	D	A	N	G	X	R	F
U	W	T	E	X	T	N	U	M	S	F	T	V	E
K	R	Y	N	C	A	M	P	A	I	G	N	b	E
C	T	F	Q	C	Y	K	I	M	Q	K	W	E	D
C	Y	B	E	R	B	U	L	L	Y	I	N	G	X

2 **Remettez les lettres dans l'ordre et écrivez la phrase cachée.**

CBREY-LULNYIBG

3		1	2	5			8	9	9		12	11	

PSTO

	10		

TIARYHC

3		4	5	12		

MOMNTCIUY

3	10			8	11	12		

Phrase cachée :

1	2

3	4	5	2	7	8	9

10	11	9	12	11	2

Challenge!

3 **Listez un maximum de réseaux sociaux et leurs principales fonctionnalités.**

Training

4 **Écrivez ces données chiffrées en toutes lettres.**

a. 22% ....

b. 2/3 ....

c. 86.3% ....

d. 1/4 ....

5 105 **Écoutez et écrivez les données chiffrées.**

a. ....

b. ....

c. ....

d. ....

6 106 **Placez l'adverbe de fréquence à l'endroit qui convient. Écoutez et vérifiez.**

a. OFTEN – I .... chat .... with my friends online.

b. ALWAYS – I .... am .... scrolling through Instagram.

c. RARELY – I .... post selfies .... on social media.

d. NEVER – I .... text .... my friends in class.

7 **Traduisez les phrases suivantes.**

a. *Ma copine prend toujours des photos.* ....

b. *Je ne me sers jamais de mon téléphone.* ....

c. *3/4 des adolescents ont Internet sur leur téléphone.* ....

d. *Mes parents ne sont jamais en ligne.* ....

e. *Les jeunes adultes donnent souvent de l'argent à des associations caritatives.* ....

8 **Remettez les éléments des questions dans l'ordre. Puis répondez aux questions en utilisant des adverbes de fréquence.**

a. surf / do / the net / you / How often / ? ....

b. you / How many times / check / do / a day / your newsfeed? ....

c. How often / you / do / scroll through / your telephone / ? ....

d. selfies / How often / do / post / you / ? ....

TIPS — LANGUAGE

Les adverbes de fréquence

Ils expriment la fréquence d'une action.

never – rarely – often – usually – always se placent avant le verbe...

I never use the internet. *Je n'utilise jamais Internet.*

... sauf quand il s'agit du verbe *be* (conjugué).

The team is always online. *L'équipe est toujours en ligne.*

Les indicateurs de fréquence

Ils se placent en début ou en fin de phrase.

I post new content two or three times a day.
Je poste du nouveau contenu deux ou trois fois par jour.

Dire et écrire les données chiffrées

Les fractions

voir rabat/couverture.

Le numérateur se lit comme un chiffre cardinal et le dénominateur se lit comme un chiffre ordinal.

1/3 a/one third *un tiers*

3/4 three quarters (GB) / fourths (US) *trois quarts*

Exception : 1/2 (a) half *un demi*

Les données chiffrées

three in ten *3 sur 10*

UNIT 9

B1

PROJECT

Conduct a Survey

About Social Networks

SCENARIO

À l'occasion de la journée des médias, vous préparez un questionnaire sur les réseaux sociaux à destination de tout public, dont vous analyserez les réponses.

A2

Réaliser un questionnaire sur les réseaux sociaux

- Choisissez le thème de votre sondage parmi les thèmes abordés dans l'unité : le cyber-harcèlement, les levées de fonds à travers les réseaux sociaux, les conséquences des problèmes liés aux réseaux sociaux, la surveillance des internautes, le nombre d'heures passées devant un écran, les réseaux sociaux et leur dépendance.
- Rédigez votre questionnaire de 5 questions avec trois réponses possibles pour chaque question et soumettez-le aux personnes que vous souhaitez interroger.

→ Theme of the survey: ....

→ Age: ☐ 15 ☐ 16 ☐ 17 ☐ 18 and over

→ Question 1: ....
....
☐ ....
☐ ....
☐ ....

→ Question 2: ....
....
☐ ....
☐ ....
☐ ....

→ Question 3: ....
....
☐ ....
☐ ....
☐ ....

→ Question 4: ....
....
☐ ....
☐ ....
☐ ....

→ Question 5: ....
....
☐ ....
☐ ....
☐ ....

B1

Rendre compte des résultats d'un sondage

- Dépouillez et analysez les résultats.
- Faites une synthèse écrite des résultats obtenus pour dégager les tendances du groupe de personnes interrogées.

Auto évaluation

PORTFOLIO

foucherconnect.fr/21ptt60

UNIT 9

Accompagnement Personnalisé

Réagir à une problématique à l'écrit

Stratégies

Lors d'une des épreuves de votre baccalauréat, vous devrez répondre à un sujet à l'écrit.
Pour répondre à une problématique, il est possible de rédiger votre présentation en 2 parties en présentant les aspects positifs et négatifs, ou les avantages et les inconvénients.

1 Faites un brainstorming ou listez vos idées. Écrivez toutes vos idées sur une feuille de brouillon, puis essayez de les classer.

2 Organisez votre propos. Hiérarchisez vos idées et séparez vos arguments de vos exemples. Au brouillon, faites des phrases courtes et simples. Utilisez des mots outils (A) et (B) ou chronologiques. Hiérarchisez vos idées et pensez à séparer vos idées, vos arguments et vos exemples. Pensez à introduire votre écrit et à conclure.

3 Mettez votre texte au propre. Recopiez votre texte au propre en soignant votre écriture. Relisez-vous et essayez de corriger les erreurs d'orthographe, de pluriels et de grammaire.

Observation

Lisez la rédaction de Paco : surlignez l'introduction et la conclusion, soulignez les arguments positifs et barrez les négatifs. Encadrez les mots outils.

Nowadays, social networks are used by many teenagers and this tool must be used with caution[1].

First of all, I think social media can be great. Facebook is a means to connect relatives[2] who live far away, you can discover new things with Instagram for instance, or just to have fun with the TikTok app.

However, on the other hand, as far as I am concerned I believe these interactions can sometimes be hard to handle for teenagers. Social networks can also be a place for cyber-bullying which can lead to depression. Some problems online can become proper problems in real life, online harassment can become real life harassment for high school teenagers, for example. In these situations, teenagers must be helped to deal with the distress.

In conclusion, social media can be both good and bad, it depends on its use.

1. *prudence* ; 2. *famille*

À vous de jouer !

À l'aide des stratégies et de ce que vous avez pu observer, répondez à la problématique suivante :

Should schools forbid mobiles?

À retenir

A Organiser une présentation	B Connecteurs logiques d'opposition
– First of all *premièrement, d'abord*	– However *cependant, toutefois*
– Secondly *deuxièmement*	– Contrary to *contrairement à*
– Thirdly *troisièmement*	– On the one hand... on the other hand *d'une part... d'autre part*
– Then, next *puis, ensuite*	– instead of *au lieu de*
– To finish *pour finir*	– nevertheless *néanmoins, toutefois*

UNIT 10 Powerful Women in History

PROJECT B1

Your school is organising an exhibition for Women's History Month to celebrate the exceptional women who have marked history. Choose a woman you admire and create a poster to explain why she is remarkable.

1 **Look at the picture and describe what you see.**

2 107 **Listen and fill in the table with the missing information.**

	a. Amelia Earhart	b. Angela Davis	c. Marilyn Monroe
Occupation	....	....	Actress / ....
Date / Period	....	1970s	....
Best known as	The .... to fly solo across the Atlantic Ocean.	The leader who fought against .... and for	The star who revolutionised ....
Personality	....	fearless[1]	.... / self-confident[2]

1. courageuse; 2. ayant confiance en soi

FLIPPED CLASSROOM

Find the words for the following definitions.

a. The right to vote: ....

b. Satisfied with oneself: ....

c. An accomplishment: ....

d. An invisible barrier that stops women's progress: ....

1'30"
CAPSULE
Powerful Women in History
foucherconnect.fr/21ptt61

UNIT 10 First Fights

ACTIVITY A Women Suffrage

LET'S GO FURTHER !!! →p. 112

1 108 **Listen and fill in the table with the missing information.**

voted in a presidential election • started the National American Woman Suffrage Association • wrote the Women's Suffrage Amendment • delivered a speech to encourage women to fight

Sojourner Truth	Elisabeth Cady Stanton	Susan B. Anthony
Women's rights activists		
....	....	
....		....
....		....
....		....

2 108 **Listen again and tick True or False.**

a. The idea of suffrage for American men started in the 1840s. ☐ True ☐ False

b. Susan B. Anthony and Elisabeth Cady Stanton were determined women. ☐ True ☐ False

c. In 1870, African-American men could vote. ☐ True ☐ False

d. In 1920, women could vote. ☐ True ☐ False

WORD BOX

- **an activist** un(e) militant(e)
- **an amendment** une loi américaine
- **the suffrage** le droit de vote

ACTIVITY B The Next Steps

1 **Read the text and write the missing titles for each paragraph.**

Go on the birth control pill[1] • Get a credit card • Get an Ivy League[2] education

1. la pilule contraceptive; 2. universités prestigieuses américaines

2 **Circle the right answer.**

a. Banks (*could* / *couldn't*) refuse to give women credit cards in 1975.

b. Women (*could* / *couldn't*) always decide not to have children before the 1960s.

c. Women (*could* / *couldn't*) study at Princeton in 1970.

d. Women (*could* / *couldn't*) study at Harvard in 1970.

Things women couldn't do in the 1960s

1. ....

In the 1960s, a bank could refuse to issue a credit card to an unmarried woman; even if she was married, her husband was required to cosign. [...] It was not until the Equal Credit Opportunity Act of 1974 that it became illegal to refuse a credit card to a woman based on her gender. [...]

2. ....

Issues like reproductive freedom and a woman's right to decide when and whether to have children were only just beginning to be openly discussed in the 1960s. [...]

3. ....

Yale and Princeton didn't accept female students until 1969. Harvard didn't admit women until 1977.

Katie McLaughlin, *CNN*, August 25, 2014.

ACTIVITY C

A Historic Marathon

1 **Look at the photo and describe orally what you see. Imagine the situation.**

GRAMMAR SPOT

a. A bank could refuse to issue a credit card.

b. Women could not vote.

c. She wasn't allowed to do it.

➡ *La phrase **a** exprime:*
- ☐ *la possibilité au passé*
- ☐ *l'interdiction au passé*

➡ *Les phrases **b** et **c** expriment:*
- ☐ *la possibilité au passé*
- ☐ *l'interdiction au passé*

Training ex. 7 & 8 p. 114

2 109 **Listen to the description and answer the questions.**

a. When was this photo taken? ....

b. What was the event? ....

c. Who is Kathrine Switzer? ....

....

3 109 **Listen again and write who these men are and what they're doing.**

He is Kathrine's ....

He is trying ....

....

He is one of the ....

....

He wanted Kathrine ....

....

4 110 **Listen to the consequences of this marathon and circle the words you hear.**

This marathon experience (*challenged / changed*) her life. In 1974, she (*was / won*) the New York City Marathon, and she (*campaigned / complained*) for the women's marathon to become an (*epic / Olympic*) sport in 1984. Her story is an (*inspiration / information*) to women: in 2017, more than (*12,300 / 1,230*) women started the Boston Marathon.

ACTION 1

Donner des informations sur des événements passés A2+

Use the information from activities A, B and C to complete the timeline and present it orally. You can add other dates and information.

1920	1967	1974	1977
....	....	....	....
....	....	....	....
....	....	....	....

UNIT 10

Wind of Change...

ACTIVITY D

... In Movies

1 **Watch the video and explain orally what you understood.**

2 **Watch the video from the beginning to 0:30 and fill in the missing words.**

2'00"
VIDÉO
Wonder Woman' Sets Record, Shatters A Hollywood Glass Ceiling
foucherconnect.fr/21ptt62

proud • female director • ceilings • empowering • achievement

We always knew she could deflect bullets. Now she's shattering .... *Wonder Woman* topped $100 million at the domestic box office. It's the largest opening weekend ever for a movie led by a ...., a momentous .... for filmmaker Patty Jenkins: "I'm so .... to be a part of something that might make a change and make you think differently." Moms and daughters flocked to the film, drawn by an .... message for women.

WORD BOX
- **dress up** se déguiser
- **a model** un modèle

3 111 **Match the words with their translation.**

a. deflect •	• 1. *dévier*
b. a female director •	• 2. *qui donne du pouvoir*
c. a ceiling •	• 3. *une réalisatrice*
d. empowering •	• 4. *un plafond*
e. shattering •	• 5. *briser*

4 **Underline the sentence which means that *Wonder Woman* is breaking an artificial barrier to success.**

*who I'm going as: *en qui je vais me déguiser*

ACTIVITY E

... In Sports

STEP BY STEP →p. 112

1 **Look at the cartoon and answer the questions.**

a. What do you see on the left side? ....

b. Are the children boys or girls? ....

c. What are they doing? ....

d. Who is Simone Biles? ....

....

e. What is the cartoon showing? ....

....

2 112 **Listen and fill in with the missing verbs.**

Simone Biles .... many World Championship and Olympic medals. She .... a book about her life and .... taking classes at the University of the People. Biles .... also .... the university's global ambassador. She .... a special scholarship[1] in her name to help students.

1. *bourse d'étude*

ACTIVITY F

... In Politics

Power of Purple and Pearls

Kamala Harris took oath as the Vice-President of the United States of America, the nation's first female VP, also the first VP of black and Indian origin. [...]

Kamala Harris wore a purple dress created by Christopher John Rogers and Sergio Hudson, two black designers. [...] Harris has broken the glass ceiling and assumed the office of US Vice-President, an office that had been the mainstay[1] of male politicians so far. [...] Purple is also intrinsically weaved into[2] the women's suffrage movement. It was a decades-long battle for the right for women to vote in the US. Purple is also linked to the story of Shirley Chisholm, the first black woman to run for the office of US President. Chisholm was also the first black woman elected to the US Congress and she was well known for using purple in her campaign flyers.

Harris also wore a pearl necklace. It was seen as an acknowledgement to her sorority, Alpha Kappa Alpha, the first intercollegiate historically African American Greek-lettered sorority. The pearls are associated with the black sisterhood that has helped her stand strong.

Vineet Sharma, www.timesnownews.com, 21 January 2021.

1. *la base, le pilier*; 2. *lié à*

1 Read the text and tick the right answer.

a. Kamala Harris is: ☐ the president of the USA ☐ the vice-president of the USA

b. It's: ☐ the first time ☐ the second time for a woman.

c. The text is about: ☐ what she said ☐ what she wore

2 Find the English for:

a. *a prêté serment* (§1): ....

b. *être candidat à* (§2): ....

c. *un signe de reconnaissance* (§3): ....

d. *son association d'étudiantes* (§3): ....

e. *la solidarité féminine* (§3): ....

GRAMMAR SPOT

a. **Harris has broken the glass ceiling.**

b. **Kamala Harris wore a purple dress.**

➜ *La phrase qui exprime une action passée dont on constate les effets dans le présent est :* ......

➜ *Le temps employé pour cette phrase est le :*

☐ *prétérit*

☐ present perfect

Training ex. 5 & 6 p. 114

3 Answer the questions.

a. Why is the election of Kamala Harris so special? ....

....

b. How has she broken the glass ceiling? ....

....

c. Why did she choose to wear purple? ....

....

d. Who is Shirley Chisholm? ....

....

....

....

e. Why did Kamala Harris choose to wear a pearl necklace? ....

....

....

ACTION 2

B1 **Comprendre une présentation**

Watch the video and explain in French why Beyoncé is considered to be a role model.

2'09"

VIDÉO Beyoncé's Most Empowering Moments

foucherconnect.fr/21ptt63

Differentiated Activities

ACTIVITY A — LET'S GO FURTHER!!!

p. 108

INTERNET
Colors of the Suffrage Movement
foucherconnect.fr/21ptt64

Search for information about Emmeline Pankhurst on this website and fill in the table.

Name	Emmeline Pankhurst
Nationality	....
Adjectives to describe her	....
What she did in 1903	....
Militant actions	....
What happened between 1908 and 1912	....

ACTIVITY E — STEP BY STEP

p. 110

1 Look at the cartoon and tick the right answers.

a. On the left, there are Halloween:
☐ statues ☐ costumes ☐ posters
such as: ☐ superheroes ☐ princesses

b. On the right, there are four: ☐ boys ☐ girls

c. They are: ☐ watching TV ☐ singing a song
☐ listening to music

d. Simone Biles is the: ☐ man ☐ woman on TV.
She is an: ☐ American ☐ European ☐ Asian
☐ singer ☐ gymnast who won a gold:
☐ medal ☐ trophy for the 25th time. It is a record.

e. The cartoon is showing that little girls want to dress up as: ☐ real people ☐ fictional characters
and not: ☐ real people ☐ fictional characters
anymore. The girls consider Simone Biles to be a:
☐ model ☐ mother

2 (113) Listen and circle the right verb.

a. Simone Biles (*has won / won*) many World Championship and Olympic medals.

b. She (*has written / wrote*) a book about her life and (*has started / started*) taking classes at the University of the People.

c. Biles (*has also become / also became*) the university's global ambassador.

d. She (*has established / established*) a special scholarship[1] in her name to help students.

1. *bourse d'étude*

UNIT 10

TRAINING

AUDIO
foucherconnect.fr/21ptt65

EXERCICES INTERACTIFS
foucherconnect.fr/21ptt66

in TUNE

A 114 **Écoutez et répétez le mot *could* en faisant attention à sa prononciation.**

B 115 **Écoutez les mots et entourez ceux qui se prononcent [ʊ] comme *could*.**

a. look b. should c. good d. women e. woman f. sisterhood g. proud h. group

1 Complétez le métier de ces femmes sous chaque image.

a. V……-P……………

b. G……………………

c. A……………………

d. M…………… R…………

e. D……………………

2 Reliez chaque adjectif à sa définition ou son synonyme.

a. proud •	• 1. when you work a lot
b. fearless •	• 2. when you feel satisfied
c. determined •	• 3. brave, courageous
d. inspirational •	• 4. ambitious
e. self-confident •	• 5. when you encourage or give hope
f. hard-working •	• 6. when you have no doubts in yourself

3 Challenge!

Faites le plus de phrases possibles en utilisant les adjectifs de l'exercice 2 et les mots de l'exercice 1.
Ex: Women's rights activists were determined to have the right to vote.

4 Rayez dans la grille la traduction des mots ci-dessous. Puis, découvrez le nom de la première femme américaine qui est allée dans l'espace avec les 9 premières lettres restantes.

E	A	S	A	L	L	Y	R	I	D	E	X	E	B	S
G	R	C	U	D	W	S	T	K	D	Y	M	E	U	L
A	G	J	H	A	D	D	Z	O	R	P	V	F	E	E
R	K	T	V	I	S	M	O	A	O	Y	F	B	M	D
F	Z	O	Z	Y	E	H	E	W	E	R	O	C	L	O
F	L	X	C	P	R	V	E	X	A	Y	U	H	R	M
U	I	T	F	E	T	R	E	G	U	K	L	A	P	L
S	B	E	T	J	I	Q	E	M	C	E	B	T	R	V
D	S	S	K	N	L	T	J	A	E	V	E	G	P	S
B	I	G	G	P	T	N	E	M	D	N	E	M	A	T
S	S	I	V	E	X	O	U	N	P	K	T	T	N	J
G	L	A	S	S	C	E	I	L	I	N	G	C	W	T
A	C	K	N	O	W	L	E	D	G	E	M	E	N	T

- droit de vote
- réussite
- plafond de verre
- modèle
- solidarité féminine
- loi américaine
- signe de reconnaissance
- qui donne du pouvoir
- nom donné aux militantes du droit de vote des femmes au Royaume-Uni.

→ ……………………………………………………
was the first American woman in space.

5 **Conjuguez chaque verbe entre parenthèses au *present perfect*.**

a. Beyoncé (defend) .... always .... women's rights in her songs.

b. She (worked) .... with many artists and (win) .... many awards.

c. Beyoncé and her husband (live) .... in Los Angeles for many years.

d. Beyoncé and other celebrities (donate) .... millions to help people in need.

6 116 **Écoutez et complétez les phrases avec les verbes manquants.**

a. Serena Williams .... many tennis tournaments.

b. Her numerous victories .... a positive influence on young girls.

c. She .... more involved in social change.

d. In 2016, she .... her support of Black Lives Matter on social media.

7 **Observez les photos et rédigez des phrases en expliquant ce que les femmes ne pouvaient pas faire dans les années 1920.**

....

....

....

....

....

8 **Traduisez les phrases ci-dessous.**

a. Les femmes ne pouvaient pas courir de marathons.

....

....

b. Les femmes pouvaient étudier à Harvard en 1978.

....

....

c. Les femmes américaines n'étaient pas autorisées à voter avant 1920.

....

....

d. Les femmes britanniques étaient autorisées à voter en 1920. ....

....

TIPS

LANGUAGE

La permission et l'interdiction au passé

***Could* est la forme de *can* au prétérit.**

In 1870, all men could vote. *En 1870, tous les hommes pouvaient voter.*

Pour exprimer l'interdiction ou l'impossibilité, on peut utiliser *could* ou *be + allowed to* à la forme négative.

Women couldn't study at Harvard in 1970. *Les femmes ne pouvaient pas étudier à Harvard en 1970.*

At that time, women were not allowed in most marathons. *À cette époque, les femmes n'étaient pas autorisées dans la plupart des marathons.*

Le prétérit vs le *present perfect*

Le prétérit exprime des événements passés et révolus.

Kamala Harris wore a pearl necklace. *Kamala Harris portait un collier de perles.*

Le *present perfect* exprime des événements commencés dans le passé dont on contate les effets dans le présent ou/et ayant un rapport avec le moment où l'on parle.

The sisterhood has helped her. *La solidarité féminine l'a aidée.*

UNIT 10

PROJECT

B1

Present an Inspirational Woman

SCENARIO

Votre lycée vous demande de participer à une exposition pour célébrer les femmes qui ont marqué l'histoire. Créez une affiche et présentez la personnalité féminine de votre choix.

A2+

Rechercher des informations factuelles et pertinentes

- Choisissez une personnalité féminine que vous admirez.
- Recherchez sur Internet des informations (éléments biographiques, réussites...) et prenez en note les éléments qui seront utiles pour votre présentation.

→ Name: ....

→ Nationality: ....

→ Date of birth (and death): ....

→ Occupation(s): ....
....

→ Main actions / fights: ....
....

→ Reasons for your choice: ....
....

A2+

Réaliser une affiche

- Recherchez des photos représentatives de la personne que vous avez choisie.
- Rassemblez les photos et organisez-les sur une affiche.
- Notez les éléments les plus pertinents sur l'affiche (dates, lieux...). Ne rédigez pas de phrases.

B1

Présenter une personnalité

- Préparez ce que vous allez dire à l'oral à l'aide des éléments que vous avez notés.
- Utilisez un dictionnaire en ligne pour vérifier la prononciation des mots nouveaux.
- Entraînez-vous à faire votre présentation orale en prenant appui sur l'affiche que vous avez créée.

Auto évaluation

PORTFOLIO

foucherconnect.fr/21ptt67

UNIT 10 Accompagnement personnalisé

Justifier ses choix

Stratégies

1 Choisissez vos arguments. Notez toutes les idées qui vous viennent à l'esprit et qui pourront expliquer le choix que vous avez fait dans votre présentation.

2 Justifiez à l'aide de vos préférences. Utilisez des expressions variées pour les exprimer A.

3 Donnez des exemples. Illustrez votre présentation par des exemples vus en cours ou liés à vos connaissances personnelles B.

4 Donnez votre avis. Utilisez des expressions pour prendre position et défendre votre point de vue C.

Observation

117 **Écoutez la présentation de Kevin sur une femme marquante et complétez le tableau.**

Expressions à retenir	Arguments
....	One of the first women to break the glass ceiling
I think	....
I like her a lot because	....
....	Politics
....	The first woman in a Presidential election

À vous de jouer !

Utilisez les arguments ci-dessous pour présenter Meghan Markle en vous inspirant des stratégies et de la rubrique Observation.

- be a free and independent woman
- choose not to follow the royal path despite her marriage with a Prince
- fight for gender equality
- help the Los Angeles inhabitants during the COVID-19 pandemic

À retenir

A Pour exprimer ses préférences

- I prefer... *Je préfère...*
- I'm very interested in... *Je suis très intéressé par...*
- I like this a lot because... *J'aime beaucoup cela parce que...*
- I'm fond of... *J'adore...*
- What strikes me the most... *Ce qui me marque le plus...*

B Pour donner des exemples

- For example/For instance... *Par exemple...*
- Such as... *Tel(le) que...*

C Pour donner son avis

- In my opinion... *À mon avis...*
- I think/believe (that)... *Je pense/crois que...*
- To me/To my mind... *Pour moi...*
- According to me... *Selon moi...*

CULTURE CLICK 5 SCARY CREATURES

A

B

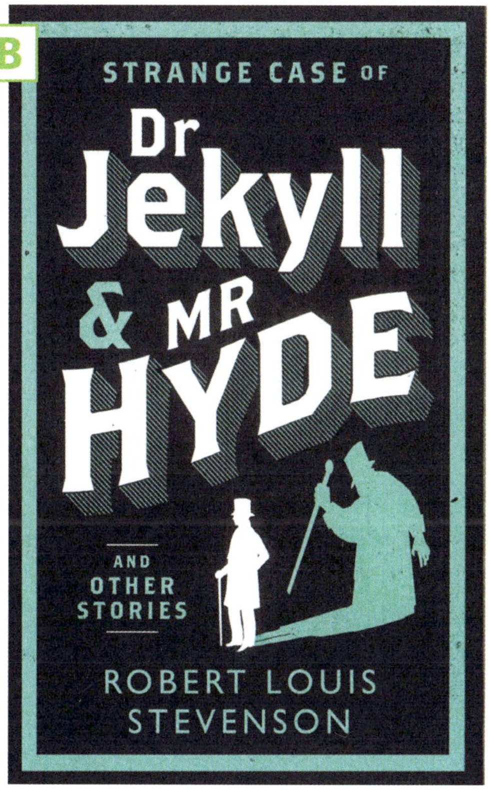

1 118 **Listen and fill in the grid.**

	A	B
Title	....	....
Author	....	....
Date	....	....
Scientist	Victor	....
Experiment with:	....	potions

2 119 **Complete the sentences with the words from the list. Then listen and check.**

humans • morality • stronger • creator • suicide • control

Both experiments go out of ...., Victor's monster kills many .... and Victor's family. Mr Hyde becomes .... than Dr Jekyll and kills several people. At the end of the story, both monsters commit .... because they can't stand* their actions.

The two monsters, created by human experimentation, question the .... and responsibility of the ....

* *supporter*

QUIZ

1. Bram Stoker wrote:
- ☐ a. Carrie
- ☐ b. Twilight
- ☐ c. Dracula

2. Captain Nemo fights:
- ☐ a. the Loch Ness monster
- ☐ b. a giant squid[1]
- ☐ c. Moby Dick

3. To frighten children, adults call:
- ☐ a. the Bogeyman[2]
- ☐ b. Bigfoot
- ☐ c. the Abominable Snowman

4. The Balrog appears in:
- ☐ a. *The Lord of the Rings*
- ☐ b. *Game of Thrones*
- ☐ c. *Harry Potter*

5. *Dracula* takes place in:
- ☐ a. Germany and England
- ☐ b. Transylvania and England
- ☐ c. Russia and England

6. The Hound of the Baskervilles is:
- ☐ a. a demon
- ☐ b. a dog
- ☐ c. a tiger

7. Beauty loves:
- ☐ a. the Beast
- ☐ b. the Toad[3]
- ☐ c. the Werewolf

8. Grendel, a man-eating monster, is killed by:
- ☐ a. Dr Van Helsing
- ☐ b. the Witcher
- ☐ c. Beowulf

9. The author of *The Werewolf of Paris* was:
- ☐ a. French
- ☐ b. Canadian
- ☐ c. American

10. The story of *Interview with the Vampire* begins in:
- ☐ a. Europe
- ☐ b. Louisiana
- ☐ c. New Orleans

1. un calamar; 2. le croquemitaine; 3. un crapaud

121 **Listen and check.**

Your score: ..../10

3 Match the descriptions and the monsters.

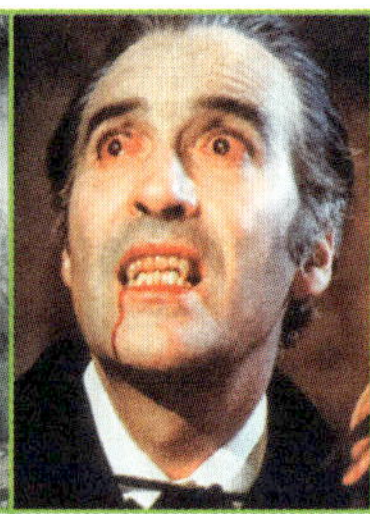

1. A gremlin (......)	2. The Bogey-man (......)	3. Dracula (......)	4. Bigfoot (......)

a. His mouth is fixed and rather cruel-looking, with peculiarly sharp[1] white teeth.

b. Some footprints[2] were found in Canada. People believe it's a giant, hairy, humanlike creature.

c. He is just about one metre tall. He has sharp teeth, large batlike ears and three sharp claws[3] on his feet and hands.

d. This diabolical entity eats naughty[4] children. He is the ally of desperate parents when their children refuse to go to bed.

1. pointues; 2. des empreintes; 3. des griffes; 4. désobéissants

4 120 Listen and underline what you hear.

a. Pennywise, the Dancing Clown, alias "It", is a creature which comes from another (*universe / planet*).

b. "It" is (*millions / billions*) of years old and it lives in Derry, (*Maryland / Maine*), USA.

c. "It" can (*morph*[1] */ change*) into any human, animal or object.

d. "It" takes the shape of the characters' (*best friends / family*) to manipulate them or lead them into a trap[2].

e. "It" is (*nervous / charming*) before attacking people.

f. Its favourite prey[3] is (*adults / children*).

g. "It" feeds on humans for a year then goes back into hibernation for about (*13 / 30*) years.

1. se métamorphoser; 2. un piège; 3. une proie

Annexes

ACTION 3

p. 35

VERS LE CCF

Les modalités d'examen en Baccalauréat Professionnel

Arrêté du 17 juin 2020 publié au Bulletin Officiel n°35 du 23 juillet 2020

▸ **Épreuve obligatoire LVA et LVB: coefficient 2 pour chaque langue vivante (sauf pour la spécialité Commercialisation et service en restauration: coefficient 3).**

▸ **Épreuve facultative: seuls les points au-dessus de 10 sont pris en compte pour le calcul de la moyenne générale.**

MODES D'ÉVALUATION

I – Contrôle en cours de formation ou épreuve ponctuelle (pour l'épreuve obligatoire)

Le contrôle en cours de formation a pour objectif de vérifier vos compétences, au niveau B1+ du CECRL pour la LVA et au niveau A2+ du CECRL pour la LVB, à:
– comprendre la langue orale;
– comprendre un document écrit;
– s'exprimer à l'écrit;
– s'exprimer à l'oral en continu;
– interagir à l'oral,
dans des situations de la vie quotidienne, sociale et professionnelle.

L'épreuve est notée sur 20, chaque partie est notée sur 4.

Le contrôle en cours de formation et l'épreuve ponctuelle sont constitués de deux situations d'évaluation: une évaluation écrite commune (situation A) et une interrogation orale individuelle (situation B).

Situation A: L'évaluation écrite commune

Durée: 1 heure, sans préparation.

- **Partie 1: compréhension de l'oral**

  À partir d'un enregistrement sonore ou vidéo n'excédant pas une minute trente, entendu et/ou visionné trois fois, vous rédigerez un compte rendu en français.

- **Partie 2: compréhension de l'écrit**

  À partir d'un support authentique en anglais n'excédant pas quinze lignes et dont la thématique, le sujet ou l'objet peut avoir un lien avec ceux du support de la partie 1, il vous faudra rédiger un compte rendu en français.

- **Partie 3: expression écrite**

  À partir de deux sujets au choix pouvant présenter un lien thématique avec les documents supports des parties 1 et 2, vous devrez réagir à une problématique d'ordre général, commenter une citation ou une affirmation ou répondre à un message écrit (lettre, courriel, post ou article de blog, etc.) en anglais.
  La longueur minimale attendue se situe entre 100 et 120 mots.

Situation B : l'épreuve orale individuelle

Durée : 10 minutes

- **Partie 1 : expression orale en continu**

  Durée : 5 minutes maximum

  Vous devrez présenter, selon votre choix :
  – un travail/projet/produit/service réalisé dans le cadre de votre scolarité et ayant fait appel à une utilisation de l'anglais ;
  – une expérience professionnelle ayant fait appel à une utilisation de l'anglais.

- **Partie 2 : expression orale en interaction**

  Durée : 5 minutes maximum

  À la suite de l'exposé de la partie 1, l'évaluateur vous posera des questions et formulera des demandes d'explications ou d'illustrations complémentaires. La conversation pourra être élargie si besoin.

II – Épreuve ponctuelle (pour l'épreuve facultative)

L'épreuve de langue vivante facultative a pour objectif de vérifier vos compétences, au niveau B1+ du CECRL, à :
– vous exprimer à l'oral en continu ;
– interagir à l'oral ;
– comprendre un document écrit.

L'épreuve, qui se déroule en trois parties, est notée sur 20 et la durée totale maximale de l'épreuve est de vingt minutes.

- **Partie 1 : expression orale en continu**

  Durée : 5 minutes maximum

  Vous devrez prendre la parole de manière continue en présentant, selon votre choix :
  - un travail/projet/produit/service réalisé dans le cadre de votre scolarité et ayant fait appel à une utilisation de l'anglais ;
  - une expérience professionnelle ayant fait appel à une utilisation de l'anglais.

- **Partie 2 : expression orale en interaction**

  Durée : 5 minutes maximum

  À la suite de l'exposé de la partie 1, l'évaluateur vous posera des questions et formulera des demandes d'explications ou d'illustrations complémentaires. La conversation pourra être élargie si besoin.

- **Partie 3 : compréhension de l'écrit**

  Durée : 10 minutes maximum

  À partir d'un support en anglais n'excédant pas quinze lignes, vous devrez répondre, à l'oral et en français, à 4 ou 6 questions graduées (du général au particulier).

COMPRÉHENSION DE L'ORAL

Durée : 10 minutes

1983: Sally Ride Is First US Woman in Space

1'59"
VIDÉO
foucherconnect.fr/21ptt68

Vous visionnerez la vidéo (→ 1'28") trois fois. Les visionnages seront espacés d'une minute. Après le troisième visionnage, vous rédigerez un compte rendu en français.

Aide à la rédaction du compte rendu

- Repérez tout d'abord les éléments suivants :

– thème principal de la vidéo : ....

– identités et informations sur les personnes : ....

....

– événement principal : ....

– autres événements importants : ....

....

– point de vue : ....

– éléments implicites du document : ....

....

– fonction du document : *relater – informer – convaincre – divertir – dénoncer – autre* ....

- Rédigez votre compte rendu sur papier libre en utilisant les éléments que vous avez notés ci-dessus.

COMPRÉHENSION DE L'ÉCRIT

Durée : 25 minutes

Lisez le texte et rédigez un compte rendu en français.

Jeff Bezos: Blue Origin Space Company Will Take First Woman To the Moon

Reuters Sat 5 Dec 2020 20:39 GMT

Jeff Bezos' space company Blue Origin will take the first woman to the moon, the billionaire said as NASA nears a decision over who will supply its first privately built lunar landers[1], meant to be capable of sending astronauts to the moon by 2024. [...]

Twelve men have walked on the Moon, but no women. NASA aims to change that, administrator Jim Bridenstine saying last year the first woman to complete a lunar landing will be drawn from the current astronaut corps. [...]

Bezos's company has vied[2] for lucrative government contracts. In the race to build NASA's system to ferry humans to the moon in the next decade, it is competing with rival billionaire Elon Musk's SpaceX and Dynetics, owned by Leidos Holdings. [...]

NASA has said it will pick two companies "in early March" 2021, to continue building lander prototypes for crewed missions beginning in 2024.

www.theguardian.com.

1. *alunisseur* ; 2. *être en concurrence pour*

Aide à la rédaction du compte rendu

• Repérez les éléments suivants :

– nature du document : *extrait d'œuvre littéraire – article de presse – publicité – lettre/courrier – autre*

– thème principal du document : ....

– identité et informations sur les personnages : ....

....

– événement principal décrit dans le document : ....

....

– autres événements importants : ....

– fonction du document : *relater – informer – convaincre – divertir – dénoncer – autre* ....

....

....

....

....

....

....

....

....

EXPRESSION ÉCRITE

Durée : 25 minutes

Vous traiterez, en anglais et en 100 à 120 mots, l'un des deux sujets suivants, au choix.

Sujet 1 : Commentez l'affirmation → *Space exploration is necessary.*

Sujet 2 : Votre patron Edward Timms vous a laissé cette note afin que vous rédigiez pour lui un courriel de demande de réservation de salle au Soho Grand Hotel.

Write an email to Soho Grand Hotel.

Object: booking of a large conference room for our Annual General Meeting in New York.

Date: April 13. Number of guests: 150

Please ask information about:
1) Price;
2) Opening hours of the conference room;
3) Catering (what is proposed: hot meals or buffet?);
4) Distance from the public transport.

....

....

....

....

....

....

....

....

COMPRÉHENSION DE L'ORAL

Durée : 10 minutes

Dresscode: First job – First Suit

1'21"
VIDÉO
foucherconnect.fr/21ptt69

Vous visionnerez la vidéo (→ 1'21") trois fois. Les visionnages seront espacés d'une minute. Après le troisième visionnage, vous rédigerez un compte rendu en français.

Aide à la rédaction du compte rendu

- Repérez tout d'abord les éléments suivants :

– 1re écoute : thème principal de la vidéo, situation (qui parle ? à qui ?) :

– 2e écoute : autres informations significatives, fonction du document :

– 3e écoute : informations plus détaillées :

COMPRÉHENSION DE L'ÉCRIT

Durée : 25 minutes

Lisez le document ci-dessous puis rédigez un compte rendu en français.

Should Your Company Adopt a Casual Dress Code?

On March 6th 2019, financial giant Goldman Sachs announced plans to relax their dress code. As a company known for its formal atmosphere and bankers dressed in suits and ties, this change was relatively unexpected as banks and financial organisations have been slow to adopt the same laid back approach to dress code as some other, more creative, sectors.

When it comes to relaxing company dress codes, Goldman Sachs is certainly not alone. Virgin Atlantic also recently changed its dress code, so female flight attendants no longer need to wear makeup and are now allowed to wear trousers. And, according to a survey by the Society for Human Resource Management, roughly 50% of companies currently have a casual dress code, a 6% increase from 2017 and 18% increase from 2014. [...]

Adopting a more relaxed dress code can have some significant benefits for your company. It can make your company more attractive to potential employees, promote gender equality, increase morale and, according to some, even boost productivity.

www.changerecruitmentgroup.com.

VERS LE CCF

Aide à la rédaction du compte rendu

- Repérez les éléments suivants :

– nature du document : ……………………………………

– thème principal du document : ……………………………………

– noms des entreprises citées : ……………………………………

– informations significatives : ……………………………………

– autres informations : ……………………………………

……………………………………

– fonction du document : ……………………………………

……………………………………
……………………………………
……………………………………
……………………………………
……………………………………
……………………………………
……………………………………
……………………………………

EXPRESSION ÉCRITE

Durée : 25 minutes

Vous traiterez, en anglais et en 100 à 120 mots, l'un des deux sujets suivants, au choix.

Sujet 1 : Répondez à la question suivante en donnant votre avis et en le justifiant avec des exemples.

→ *Do you think dress codes are important at work?*

Sujet 2 : Répondez au message de Brian.

From : brian.rogers@gmail.com
Subject: Questions about our weekend

Hi! As you know, I'm in charge of organising a great weekend with our friends next summer. I'd like to have your opinion about the place where you'd like to go and how to go there. And also, where would we take our meals? What attractions would you like to visit? What other activities would you prefer? Thank you for your answers. Any other suggestions will be welcome.

Brian

……………………………………
……………………………………
……………………………………
……………………………………
……………………………………
……………………………………
……………………………………
……………………………………
……………………………………
……………………………………

VERS LE CCF

COMPRÉHENSION DE L'ORAL

Durée : 10 minutes

Are Video Games BAD For You?

2'42"
VIDÉO
foucherconnect.fr/21ptt70

Vous visionnerez la vidéo (→ 1'06") trois fois. Les visionnages seront espacés d'une minute. Après le troisième visionnage, vous rédigerez un compte rendu en français.

Aide à la rédaction du compte rendu

- Avant les écoutes : observez le titre et émettez des hypothèses quant au sujet traité : ……………………………………………………
- Pendant ou après chaque écoute : complétez le tableau.

Thème principal et nom de l'émission	Information principale	Recommandations	Fonction / message de la vidéo
……………………	……………………	……………………	……………………

……………………………………………………………………………………

COMPRÉHENSION DE L'ÉCRIT

Durée : 25 minutes

Lisez le document ci-dessous puis rédigez un compte rendu en français.

The Benefits: Positive Effects of Video Games

1. Problem solving and logic. When a child plays a game such as *Angry Birds* [...], he trains his brain to come up with creative ways to solve puzzles and other problems [...].

2. Hand-eye coordination, fine motor and spatial skills. In shooting games, the character may be running and shooting at the same time. [...] This process requires a great deal of eye-hand coordination and visual-spatial ability to be successful. [...] There have been even studies with adults showing that experience with video games is related to better surgical skills. Also, a reason given by experts as to why fighter pilots of today are more skillful is that this generation's pilots are being weaned on* video games.

3. Planning, resource management and logistics. The player learns to manage resources that are limited, and decide the best use of resources, the same way as in real life. [...] Notably, The American Planning Association [...] and Maxis, the game creator, have claimed that *SimCity* has inspired a lot of its players to take a career in urban planning and architecture.

www.raisesmartkid.com.

* *nourris aux*

Aide à la rédaction du compte rendu

- Repérez les éléments suivants :

– nature du document : ……………………

– thème principal du document : ……………………

– noms ou genres des jeux cités : ……………………

– métiers évoqués : ……………………

– compétences développées dans le jeu : ……………………

……………………

– fonction du document : ……………………

……………………

EXPRESSION ÉCRITE

Durée : 25 minutes

Vous traiterez, en anglais et en 100 à 120 mots, l'un des deux sujets suivants, au choix.

Sujet 1 : Répondez à la question suivante → *Do you think video games are dangerous?*

Sujet 2 : Répondez au message de Thomas.

From : thknut5@gmail.com

Subject: Your training period

Dear Katy,

It was wonderful having you in the company for your training period.

Due to my schedule, we couldn't debrief your stay, so could you kindly send me what you thought about your experience? What did you think of the tasks you were given?
Did you like the atmosphere?
What were the good and bad points?

Yours sincerely,

Thomas Knut

……………………

Crédits iconographiques

Rabat .... ph © Daniel leal-Olivas/Afp

9 hg .... ph © Electronic Arts/DR
9 hd .... ph © Enix Corporation/DR
9 mg .... ph © Epic Games/DR
9 md .... ph © Playground Games/DR
9 bg .... ph © Paradox Interactive/DR
9 bd .... ph © Bandai Namco Entertainement/DR
10 h .... ph © Electronic Arts/DR
10 bg .... ph © Rockstar Games
10 bd .... ph © Electronic Arts/DR
11 h .... ph © Sony Interactive Entertainement/DR
11 b .... ph © Enix Corporation/DR
12 .... ph © Enix Corporation/DR
13 h .... ph © Nintendo/DR
13 b .... ph © Nintendo/DR
14 h .... ph © Sony Interactive Entertainement/DR
14 b .... ph © Nintendo/DR
16 h .... ph © Playstation/DR
16 m .... ph © Playstation/DR
18 .... ph © Enix Corporation/DR
19 hg .... ph © Darren Walsh/Chelsea FC/Getty Images
19 hd .... ph © Fred Duval/FilmMagic/Getty Images
19 bg .... ph © Merlin Entertainements/DR
21 m .... ph © Booklage
22 1 .... ph © Thinkstock/Getty Images
22 3 .... ph © Deejpilot/Getty Images
22 4 .... ph © Cinoby/Getty Images
22 5 .... ph © photo75/Getty Images
22 6 .... ph © Memitina/Getty Images
22 7 .... ph © mkos83/Getty Images
22 8 .... ph © ChrisSteer/Getty Images
22 9 .... ph © NicolasMcComber/Getty Images
22 10 .... ph © TomasSereda/Getty Images
23 a .... ph © william87/Getty Images
23 b .... ph © MarioGuti/Getty Images
23 d .... ph © Drazen/Getty Images
25 c .... ph © Skynesher/Getty Images
25 d .... ph © Regara/Getty Images
29 hm .... ph © Sputnik/Afp
29 hd .... ph © Nasa
29 bg .... ph © Nasa
29 bm .... ph © Nasa
29 m .... ph © Nasa
29 bd .... ph © Nasa
30 h .... ph © Nasa
35 hd .... ph © Alamy
35 a .... ph © FluxFactory/Getty Images
35 c .... ph © Curto - stock.adobe.com
37 d .... ph © Kritchanut/Getty Images
37 (4) .... ph © Pakphoto - stock.adobe.com
38 .... ph © Photodisc /Getty Images
41 .... ph © Paris 2024
42 a .... ph © The Toronto Rock
42 b .... ph © The Dallas Cowboys
42 c .... ph © The Australian Diamonds
42 d .... ph © South Africa Cricket
43 h .... ph © Shaun Botterill/Getty Images
43 b .... ph © Jeff Overs/BBC News & Current Affairs/Getty Images
44 h .... ph © Polarisimages
47 d .... ph © Geogif/Getty Images
50 .... ph © Mike Ehrmann/Getty Images/Afp
51 .... ph © FBI
52 h .... ph © FBI National Academy
52 b .... ph © Patrick Aventurier/Gamma-Rapho/Getty Images
53 .... ph © Istock/Getty Images
63 .... ph © Richard Heathcote/Getty Images/Afp
64 b .... ph © Ronald Cortes/Getty Images
64 c .... ph © Kevin Winter/Getty Images/Afp
64 e .... ph © Chiang Ying-ying/Ap/Sipa
64 b .... ph © Samir Hussein/WireImage/Getty Images
65 h .... ph © Ben Stansall/Pool/Afp
66 h .... ph © Joe Heller, PoliticalCartoons.com
66 mg .... ph © Bettmann/Getty Images
66 m .... ph © Kimberly White/Reuters
66 md .... ph © Justin Sullivan/Getty Images/Afp
67 .... ph © Oakbank Balhannah CFS/ Ap/Sipa
68 a .... ph © Laurence Griffiths/Getty Images/Afp
68 b .... ph © Harry How/Getty Images/Afp
68 d .... ph © William West/Afp
68 e .... ph © Vincenzo Pinto/Afp
68 f .... ph © Clive Masson/Getty Images /Afp
70 m .... ph © Paul Hennessy/NurPhotoAfp
73 m .... ph © Julian Calder/Governor General of New Zealand
73 g .... ph © Chris Jackson Collection/Getty Images
73 d .... ph © Hulton Archive/Getty Images
74 b .... ph © Ben Stansall/Afp
75 .... ph © Francesca Coati/Istock/Getty Images
77 h .... ph © Center for Powerful Public Schools
79 h .... ph © Hugo Félix - stock.adobe.com
85 .... ph © Lan Kogal - stock.adobe.com
86 h .... ph © StitchFix
86 b .... ph © Kinderbeauty
95 md .... ph © John Springer Coll/Corbis/Getty Images
95 bg .... ph © CBW/Alamy Stock Photo
95 bd .... ph © Rob Loud/Getty Images/Afp
96 b .... ph © Fotos International/Getty Images
98 h .... ph © CDC
99 h .... ph © rawpixel.com - stock.adobe.com
100 .... ph © Netflix/DR
107 .... ph © Brian Lopez-Santos/B2rianLS
108 hg .... ph © Hulton Archive/Getty Images
108 hm .... ph © Everett/CSU/Bridgeman images
108 hd .... ph © Nara/Getty images
109 h (reprise bg, bd) ... ph © Bettmann/Getty Images
110 m .... ph © Joe Heller, PoliticalCartoons.com
111 h .... ph © Stringer/Sputnik/Afp
113 a .... ph © Saul Loeb/Afp
113 b .... ph © Kunihiko Miura/The Yomiuri Shimbun/Afp
113 c .... ph © Universal Images Group Editorial/Getty Images
113 b .... ph © Nasa
117 hg .... DR
117 hd .... DR
118 hmg .... ph © Ezyjoe / Alamy
118 hmd .... ph © The Kobal Collection/Aurimages
118 b .... DR

Autres crédits .... stock.adobe.com

02-NB-CB/EG

PAPIER À BASE DE FIBRES CERTIFIÉES

FOUCHER s'engage pour l'environnement en réduisant l'empreinte carbone de ses livres. Celle de cet exemplaire est de : 750 g éq. CO_2
Rendez-vous sur www.editions-foucher-durable.fr

Achevé d'imprimer en Italie par L.E.G.O. S.p.A. - Lavis (TN)
Dépôt légal: 16172-0/03 - Janvier 2023